Negotiating

In life you don't get what you deserve, you get what you negotiate.

Negotiating

McGraw-Hill

New York   San Francisco   Washington, D.C.   Auckland   Bogotá
Caracas   Lisbon   London   Madrid   Mexico City   Milan
Montreal   New Delhi   San Juan   Singapore   Sydney   Tokyo   Toronto

Other *First Books for Business* include:

Budgeting and Finance

Business Presentations and Public Speaking

Sales and Marketing

Supervising and Managing People

This book is printed on acid-free paper.

Library of Congress Cataloging-in-Publication Data

Engel, Peter H., 1935–
    Negotiating / Peter H. Engel.
        p.   cm.—(First books for business)
    Includes index.
    ISBN 0-07-001566-X
    1. Marketing—Management. 2. Communication in marketing.
    3. Negotiation in business. I. Title. II. Series.
    HF5415.13.E53   1996
    658.4—dc20   96-7828
                                        CIP

1 2 3 4 5 6 7 8 9 0 DOW/DOW 9 0 1 0 9 8 7 6

ISBN 0-07-001566-X

Developed for McGraw-Hill by Affinity Communications Corp., 144 N. Robertson Blvd., Suite 103, Los Angeles, CA 90048

Conceptual Development by Mari Florence Editorial and Frank Loose Design

Designer: Frank Loose Design
Developmental Editor: Mari Florence
Production Editor: Nancy McKinley
Technical Consultant: Robert Moskowitz

Table of Contents

How to Use This Book viii

Chapter 1: Preparation

The Win-Win Approach 2

Dealing with Non-Negotiable Items 4

Know What You Want to Achieve. 6

Making the Most of a Weak Position 8

What to Give Up and When. 10

Your Personal Clock. 12

Chapter 2: Assess Your Opponent

Know Who's Across the Table 14

What Is the Context for Negotiations?. 16

Assess Your Opponent's Strengths and Weaknesses 18

Chapter 3: Negotiating Tactics

Trade One Concession for Another 20

Communicate Clearly. 22

Gain the Value of Intelligent Listening 24

Ask All the Key Questions 26

Make Your Arguments Persuasive 28

Make Sure the Other Side Hears You 30

Control Your Side's Communication. 32

The Power of Deadlines 34

Keep Your Expectations Reasonable 36

Get What You Really Want 38

Timing Is Everything! 40

Making a Fair Deal. 42

Use Your Home Court Advantage 44

Negotiating by Telephone 46

Chapter 4: Negotiating Savvy

What's Your Negotiating Style? 48

After You, I Insist 50

Small Concessions Can Make You a Winner. 52

"Worst-Case" Scenarios 54

Control the Conference Setting 56

Stay Focused on Your Goals 58

Creative Problem Solving. 60

Getting Comfortable with Acceptable Risk. 62

The Art of Conciliation. 64

The Art of Debate 66

The Art of Persuasion 68

Body Language. 70

Know When It's Time to Quit 72

Chapter 5: Negotiating Skills

Good Guy/Bad Guy Role-Playing 74

Stonewalling 76

Bluffing. 78

Bad Temper 80

Intimidation. 82

Take It or Leave It. 84

It's OK to Walk 86

Splitting the Difference. 88

Piece by Piece. 90

The Surprise Advantage. 92

Saving Face When You're Wrong 94

Turning Around a Losing Trend. 96

Playing Hunches and Insight 98

Managing the Other Side's Feelings of Success. 100

Appendix

Glossary. 103

Resources. 107

Other Books In the Series 109

Index. 113

Credits 117

Notes. 118

How to Use This Book

We created *First Books for Business* to provide answers to your most pressing questions. In developing this series, we brought together an expert panel of top-notch businesspeople who shared with us their flair for success.

By taking the best of this wealth of information and presenting it in 50 colorful two-page chapters, you'll be able to easily understand the most important elements of the art of doing business. Each chapter features special information elements where you can find help to gain a deeper understanding of the discussed topic. Here's how to best use this book:

1 *Inside Info*
Check out this feature to go behind the scenes and learn what the real pros already know!

2 *Words to Live By*
Read these inspirational, witty, or tongue-in-cheek observations that you can use to motivate yourself—or just for fun.

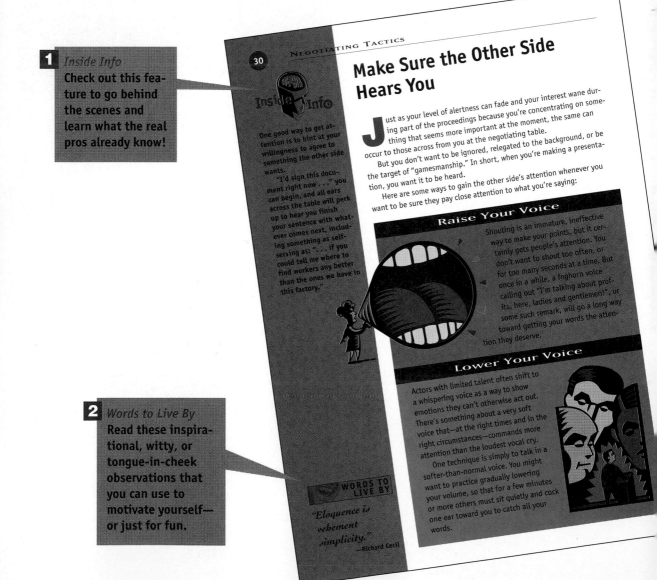

30   NEGOTIATING TACTICS

Inside Info

One good way to get attention is to hint at your willingness to agree to something the other side wants.

"I'd sign this document right now . . ." you can begin, and all ears across the table will perk up to hear you finish your sentence with whatever comes next, including something as self-serving as: ". . . if you could tell me where to find workers any better than the ones we have in this factory."

Make Sure the Other Side Hears You

Just as your level of alertness can fade and your interest wane during part of the proceedings because you're concentrating on something that seems more important at the moment, the same can occur to those across from you at the negotiating table.

But you don't want to be ignored, relegated to the background, or be the target of "gamesmanship." In short, when you're making a presentation, you want it to be heard.

Here are some ways to gain the other side's attention whenever you want to be sure they pay close attention to what you're saying:

Raise Your Voice

Shouting is an immature, ineffective way to make your points, but it certainly gets people's attention. You don't want to shout too often, or for too many seconds at a time. But once in a while, a foghorn voice calling out "I'm talking about profits, here, ladies and gentlemen!", or some such remark, will go a long way toward getting your words the attention they deserve.

Lower Your Voice

Actors with limited talent often shift to a whispering voice as a way to show emotions they can't otherwise act out. There's something about a very soft voice that—at the right times and in the right circumstances—commands more attention than the loudest vocal cry.

One technique is simply to talk in a softer-than-normal voice. You might want to practice gradually lowering your volume, so that for a few minutes or more others must sit quietly and cock one ear toward you to catch all your words.

WORDS TO LIVE BY

"Eloquence is vehement simplicity."
—Richard Cecil

Each chapter may also feature these elements:

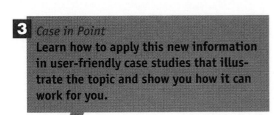

A ttempt to avoid the arbitration stage of the negotiation process. Simply put, no one wins when an outside party decides your fate. Savvy negotiators abide by this simple fact and bring their flexibility along when sitting down at the bargaining table.

TimeSaver
If your organization has done business with this opponent in the past, pull records of the past negotiations to see how your predecessors dealt with similar issues.

3 *Case in Point*
Learn how to apply this new information in user-friendly case studies that illustrate the topic and show you how it can work for you.

31

Make Sure the Other Side Hears You

SITUATION
Negotiating for Lower Purchase Price

OFFER
Will Price Be Adjusted for Long-Term Order?

COMPROMISE
Opponent Chooses Long-Term Over Short-Term Interests

IN POINT
Many of the greatest speakers in history—from Frederick Douglass to John F.
...ve utilized strong personal points to influence their au-...
...irecting your pitch to an area your opponent will be...
...sive to, you stand a greater chance of persuading the...
...o meet your terms.
...negotiating for a lower purchase price from your oppo-...
...ample, you may want to put it in terms of overall quan-...
...an do this easily by simply saying, "I'd like to purchase...
...s from you over the long run, but I just can't commit to...
...e."
... opponent wants your long-term business, he or she will...
...y to compromise to meet your terms.

Touch on the Hottest Topic
During protracted negotiations, it's impossible for everyone to maintain full alertness all the time. You can snap them to attention, however, with a verbal cracking of the whip. All you must do is somehow weave into your presentation or discussion a sentence or two about the single most important topic in these on-going negotiations.

Put on a Demonstration
Just like a picture, a demonstration is very often worth a thousand words. To get more attention for your ideas and arguments, practice putting them in vivid, visual terms that you can act out, demonstrate, or otherwise illustrate when those across the table starting putting their heads in their hands. Starting collecting interesting props, noise-makers, ideas for surprising situations, and other potential attention-getters. Try to prepare at least one for each negotiation in which you participate.

6 *Red Alert!*
Watch out for this icon! This tells you situations to avoid, things *not* to do, and red flags you should be looking for.

7 *TimeSaver*
Look here for shortcuts to getting the job done and insider tips on time management.

5 *Related Topics*
See other pages to learn more new and challenging ways of doing business.

RELATED TOPICS
➤ Make Your Arguments Most Persuasive, (pages 28–29)

4 *Skill Builders*
Practice—and master—a new skill that will help you better understand and apply the information you've learned in this book.

The Win-Win Approach

Inside Info

The "win-win" approach relies on each side working to help the other meet its objectives. As a general rule, couch your discussions in "If then . . ." terms—for example, "If you concede to us on item one, we'll give in to your item two." This give-and-take strategy enables both parties to meet on the finer points, thus moving forward toward their larger goals.

In the Middle Ages, disputes were often settled by armor-clad knights bearing heavy wooden lances and riding full-tilt at each other. The winner was whoever remained standing at the end of the battle. Not surprisingly, each side's goal was to keep the other from winning.

Today, we recognize that this head-on type of conflict wastes a lot of time. Negotiations that expend valuable energy trying to outwit, undermine, and otherwise defeat the other party benefit neither side. Experience has proven time and again that the most beneficial negotiations are those in which all parties get as much of what they want as possible—where both sides "win."

Different Ways to "Win-Win"

There are many different ways to pursue a "win-win" approach in your negotiations.

You can:

1 Ask for what is fair, remembering that negotiations which produce lopsided victories tend to break down more quickly than reasonable, equitable arrangements.

2 Maintain flexibility in your own demands and interests, making it easier for the other side to be flexible as well.

WORDS TO LIVE BY

"It is easy to be popular. It is not easy to be just."
—Rose Bird

> "What are you looking for here?"

Strategy

Ask the other side what it really wants. The most difficult problems often can be tackled by sidestepping the ancillary negotiating points and focusing instead on the other side's primary objective. Practice asking, "What are you looking for here?" or "How can we come to terms on this point?" or "What's your bottom line on this item?" at least three times during negotiations, and take note of how the responses vary during the process.

> "How can we come to terms on this point?"

> "What's your bottom line on this item?"

Be cautious with those parties who appear inflexible and unwilling to compromise. If your opponent is unyielding, your compromises and concessions won't be met with fair responses, and you could quickly end up on the losing side of the negotiations.

3 Listen to what the other side wants, and make efforts to meet their requests.

4 Compromise on the main issues so that both sides can begin to attain their goals.

5 Seek trade-offs or item-swaps so that each side gets something for everything they give up.

RELATED TOPICS

➤ Communicate Clearly, (pages 22–23)

➤ Managing the Other Side's Feelings of Success, (pages 100–101)

Dealing with Non-Negotiable Items

It seems a paradox that a book on negotiation would cover non-negotiable items. Yet negotiable and non-negotiable items are both very much a part of any negotiation.

Why? Because:

1 Non-negotiable issues have the effect of forcing the parties to be more flexible regarding issues that *are* negotiable.

2 A smart negotiator realizes that complaints about the other side's non-negotiable items serve as powerful bargaining levers—even if the negotiator doesn't really care much about how these matters turn out on their own merits.

3 Although reasonable people can vehemently disagree about negotiable items, non-negotiable items are far more likely to create an impasse and destroy any hope of the two sides reaching an agreement.

Your ability to handle non-negotiable items—both to downplay and disguise your own and to use the other party's to your best possible advantage—is a critical skill in high-powered negotiations.

Dealing with Non-negotiable Items

When *you* find an issue the *other side* doesn't want to negotiate, it's often very fruitful to:

- Focus time and energy on this issue, particularly on why the other party is not interested in negotiating it;

- Make this issue as central as possible to the entire negotiation;

- Keep coming back to the other party's refusal to negotiate this issue, both as evidence of its unwillingness to bargain fairly, and also as evidence that you're being asked to give up more than the other side.

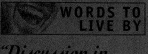

Maintaining Silence

Don't make public your own non-negotiable items. The other side will only try to use them against you any way they can. Instead, try to avoid mentioning any items you'd rather not negotiate.

At the same time, however, try to determine the other side's non-negotiable items, both by process of elimination—listing all possible issues and seeing which ones they avoid discussing—and by testing the waters—briefly naming an entirely new issue, from time to time, and then evaluating the other side's response.

Although there may be many issues you'd rather not negotiate, it's often very dangerous to entirely rule out discussion on any particular issue. Why? Because the very nature of negotiations creates the possibility that you can trade flexibility on an issue near and dear to your heart for an important concession that actually makes the overall result better for *you*.

What's more, holding firm on an issue without even the pretense of negotiating generally inflames the passions of your negotiating opponent, gives him or her motivation to fight harder on other fronts, and makes it more difficult for you to position yourself as reasonable on issues that are important to you.

TimeSaver
It's easier and faster to find issues the other side won't discuss by comparing your list of important issues to those already covered. What remains may well include some items your opponent doesn't want to talk about. Just to be safe, though, consider what other matters haven't surfaced that may also be non-negotiable for those sitting across the table.

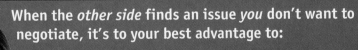

When the *other side* finds an issue *you* don't want to negotiate, it's to your best advantage to:

- Change the subject to another issue, either one you're presently negotiating or one the other side won't negotiate;

- Deny that the issue is non-negotiable but suggest you discuss it after you deal with another, more pressing issue;

- Pretend to negotiate the issue but make your demands for concessions as difficult as possible for the other side to meet;

- Negotiate the issue, but only if the other side in return negotiates one of its non-negotiable points.

RELATED TOPICS

➤ Ask All the Key Questions, (pages 26–27)

Knowing what you want from a negotiation session depends on two factors: understanding what's possible and evaluating what's important.

As part of your preparation for negotiations, be sure to:

• Make a list of all the things you'd like to achieve from it.

• For each item, create a "fall back" level of results that you will readily accept when and if it's offered.

Know What You Want to Achieve

No football coach would allow his team to face an opponent without a "game plan." No military leader would allow his forces to enter an engagement without a "battle plan." Why? Because knowing what you want to achieve, and how you expect to achieve it, constitutes an invaluable form of preparation that is absolutely necessary for making the best possible real-time decisions, situational assessments, and continual adjustments inevitably demanded when people go face-to-face with different agendas.

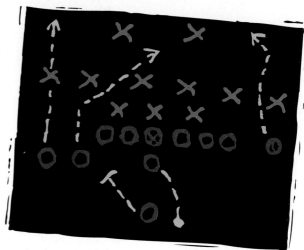

Without a clear sense of what you *want* from a negotiation, it's far too easy for you to be tempted to agree to much less than you could reasonably hope to attain. With a clear goal, however, you have a much better sense of when to push harder, when to hold firm, and when you can agree to an offer.

Developing Your List of Demands

Keep a file of important issues that you—and those you represent—want to negotiate. Note the results you want to achieve for each issue. Update and amend this file whenever you get a new idea, or whenever a situation changes in a way that seems to warrant renegotiation.

Base your negotiating position on long-term thinking, reflecting, and discussing rather than on whatever few ideas you can develop during a last-minute, high-pressure meeting.

WORDS TO LIVE BY

"In the heat of action, men are likely to forget where their best interests lie."

—Mr. Gutman, the evil "Fat Man" in *The Maltese Falcon*

Preparation

There are three possible strategies that can be used to develop your list of demands prior to entering a negotiation. Your selection of a strategy style depends on many factors in the negotiation process. Rest assured that it's very unlikely you'll ever get more than you ask for.

First, you can try to anticipate the other party's point of view, needs, goals, problems, and personality. Then you can formulate a compromise position that you feel will be "fair" to all involved.

Second, you can ask for the moon, as well as the sun, the stars, and the sky!

Third, you can create a set of demands that ask the other party for the bare minimum on which you can survive.

TimeSaver

Write your main negotiating targets on a single 3" x 5" card and keep it with you during the negotiations. As you work toward points of agreement, refer frequently to the card. This will help you focus your time and energy on your goals, without having to take a lot of time reviewing more formal position papers.

Of course, you'll want to review all the details in your negotiation position papers at least once, just before you sign off on a point, to make sure you're not giving up on an important detail due to the intensity of the negotiations.

RELATED TOPICS

➤ Get What You Really Want, (pages 38–39)

Making the Most of a Weak Position

Simply defined, the more sources from which you can obtain what you want, the stronger your position; and the fewer such options you have, the weaker your position.

For example, your position has inherent weakness when you're negotiating to keep a great job, to buy from a sole supplier or sell to a sole customer, or to obtain a loan from the only lender interested in talking with you.

But while most negotiating positions will often contain some element of weakness, there's no reason to give in to any and every demand a negotiating opponent in a stronger position may make.

Instead, seek to turn every discussion of your weaknesses into a discussion of your opponent's weaknesses. If you don't know what they are, find out; then if you need to, hammer away at them as often and as heavily as you are able. Remember, your opponent may need you as much as you need him or her. That's why it's important to overcome the weaknesses of your own position and negotiate in good faith for what you want.

WORDS TO LIVE BY

"Let us never negotiate out of fear, but let us never fear to negotiate."

—John F. Kennedy

Strategy

There are differences between real and perceived strengths and weaknesses. In many negotiations, the latter is almost as good as the former. When the other side suggests anything that amounts to "you have no place else to go," you reply with a smile, and continue negotiating as if you really do have options. This technique will often create doubt in the minds of your negotiating opponents and get you concessions you'd never achieve if you acknowledge the weakness of your position and rely on your negotiating opponent's "kind heart."

Because negotiating from a weak vantage point is extremely difficult, avoid being forced into this type of situation. You can take steps before the negotiations even begin by recognizing—and then addressing—the issues that weaken your position. You may not be able to change these sensitive issues, but you may be more prepared to put a positive spin on them and thus prevent your opponent from capitalizing on your weaknesses.

Three ways to strengthen your weak position are:

Determine how much your opponent needs your product or service. If they've entered the negotiations only because company policy dictates a review period, your opponent may be negotiating with you only as a formality. However, if they genuinely need what you have to offer, you may be in a better position than you think.

Improve your position by temporarily modifying your product or service. For example, if your product is priced higher than the competition—even if it's of higher quality—you may want to temporarily reduce the price point to make your organization look more appealing.

Imply that there is other interest in your product or service. If your opponent believes that you can meet your objectives with another organization, it may motivate them to more equitably negotiate with you than if you have no options.

TimeSaver

If your organization has done business with this opponent in the past, pull records of the past negotiations to see how your predecessors dealt with similar issues.

RELATED TOPICS

➤ Assess Your Opponents' Strengths and Weaknesses, (pages 18–19)

➤ "Worst-Case" Scenarios, (pages 54–55)

What to Give Up and When

In previous pages, we demonstrated the importance of knowing what you want to achieve. It's just as important, however, to be clear about what you're willing to give up.

To do this, put your idealized list of results in priority order according to their true importance to you and your group's overall success, well-being, and satisfaction.

List all the possible concessions you can make on each issue, and evaluate the impact of each one.

During the negotiations, you'll nearly always encounter times when the burden falls on you to offer a compromise or concession. When this occurs, you can check over your list and then make a counteroffer that effectively reduces your demand one notch on your lowest-priority objective.

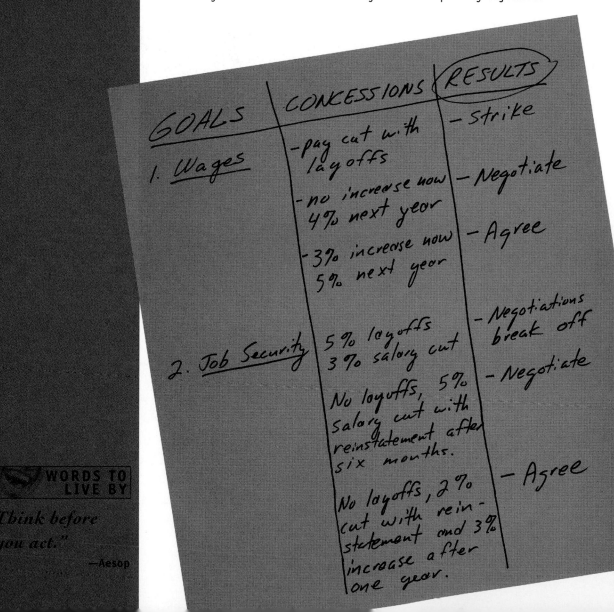

Body Language

Keep your verbal and nonverbal arguments in alignment. For example, don't speak confidently of your ability to meet the other side's terms on a particular point while puffing on a cigarette or otherwise conveying nervousness.

It takes iron discipline and a great deal of practice to make your body project the same message as your voice. But it's a skill you can learn and use to great effect in even the toughest of negotiations.

CASE IN POINT

Imagine you're faced with a need to compromise, and you use a bored or disrespectful tone of voice to say something like: "OK, fine, we'll give up one coffee break per day." Then you toss your notes on the table and slump back in your chair with an indifferent expression on your face.

It would be very easy for your negotiating opponent to interpret all these signals as proof that you simply don't care very much about giving up that coffee break.

But imagine, instead, that you use an intense, restrained, very precise tone of voice to say something like: "We were hoping to hold onto this, but since you're giving up so much we'll give up one coffee break per day." Then you clench your notes tightly in both hands and lean forward, studying your negotiating opponent's reaction like an accused murderer watching the judge opening the jury's written verdict.

The sooner you learn to treat every tiny bargaining chip like it was the key to Fort Knox, the sooner you'll become a tougher, more successful negotiator.

RELATED TOPICS

➤ Trade One Concession for Another, (pages 20–21)

Your Personal Clock

The Hustler is a classic movie showcasing the talents of both Paul Newman and Jackie Gleason. Early on, their two characters go through a major confrontation in which—at a crucial moment—Jackie Gleason's character goes to the washroom, freshens himself up, and returns to whip Paul Newman's character in a high-stakes game of billiards.

Although this was a fictional encounter, it clearly and accurately depicts the importance of fatigue and appearance in any sort of interpersonal encounter, particularly negotiations.

No one denies that as you move up the stakes of particular negotiations, they become more formalized and more carefully orchestrated.

Yet, fundamentally, negotiations are between people, who all have good and bad days, get tired, and respond to the appearance and demeanor of those across the table.

That's why it's important, at a minimum, to insulate your own side from the dangers of fatigue and intimidation. There are several ways to accomplish this.

One good way is to monitor and control the schedule to make sure fatigue is never a factor. Another way is to have a negotiating team—just like a tag team of professional wrestlers—who can take turns and keep the discussion going even when one member of the team must take a temporary breather.

Timeline of Daily Biorhythms

7–8 A.M.
A consistent time of waking each day is the best way to maximize your body's energy.

11 A.M.
The best time to schedule a meeting. Short-term memory is at its peak, as are the skills of logic and reasoning.

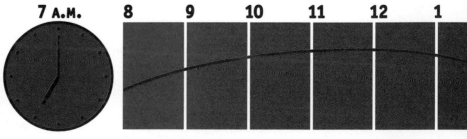

7 A.M.   **8**   **9**   **10**   **11**   **12**   **1**

9 A.M.
Good time for tackling tough projects such as organizing, planning, thinking, creating, and editing.

Noon
Complex decision-making skills are at their peak.

RED ALERT!

- Monitor the negotiations process by means of a time log. Note the beginning and ending times of all bargaining sessions, meals, and rest intervals. Call a halt to the proceedings whenever the negotiations seems to be leaving little room for proper amounts of food, drink, and rest.

  Generally, make sure you take care of your physical body's needs, so that your mind remains sharp enough to negotiate forcefully for what your side wants.

- Team negotiations can create unsatisfactory results if one member fails to keep informed as to what other members have discussed, stated, and agreed to. There can also be problems if one team member is a less forceful negotiator than another, and gets cornered by the opposition into agreeing to terms that other team members would have successfully opposed.

  To help in safeguarding against such a dilemma, have a team captain who must sign off on any agreements before they become valid, or use a total-team approach where no single member of the negotiating team has sole power to agree to any specific terms.

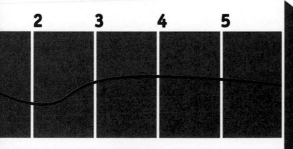

Visualizing

Practice visualizing negotiators from the other side in basic, human conditions. Imagine your negotiating opponents sleeping, eating, using the bathroom, washing up, slipping on ice, or doing anything else that makes you realize their humanity and vulnerability.

These visualizations are very effective counterweights to the expensive clothing, vast entourages, carefully cultured mannerisms, and other appearance factors that might otherwise put you at a mental and emotional disadvantage during negotiations.

2 P.M.
At this time, the body takes a dip. Many people tend to get drowsy, and performance skills decrease.

5 P.M.
Hand-eye coordination is at its best. This is a good time to leave work and go exercise.

2 3 4 5

6 P.M.

3:30 P.M.
Alertness returns. This a good time to tackle small projects such as making lists, returning phone calls, and writing letters. Long-term memory is at its highest during this period.

RELATED TOPICS

➤ Use Your Home Court Advantage, (pages 44–45)

Inside Info

When negotiating with an outside organization, it's useful to talk to competitors or analysts within the industry. These "experts" will usually know the organization's Achilles heel—if it has one—and how best to expose or exploit it. The more information you can gather about the other side, the further you can shift the balance of power toward your side of the table.

WORDS TO LIVE BY

"In dealing with cunning persons, we must ever consider their ends, to interpret their speeches; and it is good to say little to them, and that which they least look for."

—Francis Bacon

Know Who's Across the Table

Ondescending
Confident
Scared
Powerful
Honest   Amiable
Weak   Persuasive
Aggressive
Manipulative

One of the simplest yet most often overlooked ways to get better results from negotiations is to research the entity and the person(s) with whom you are negotiating. The better equipped you are with information, the more easily you can sidestep your opponents' best weapons and navigate around any problems or difficulties they throw at you.

If you're dealing with a company, it's important to explore its history, mission, organizational culture, and financial position. Don't forget, however, that even the largest organization is represented by one or more real people. What you know about them—as individuals—can be crucial in obtaining more of what you want.

Before you delve into negotiations, try to find out the answers to the following critical questions:

Know the Organization

Why is the organization negotiating? What does it hope to gain? And what is it afraid of losing?

How strong is the organization right now, in terms of its financial power, its market position, its human resources, its managerial knowledge, and its overall "savvy"?

What are the trends in the organization's industry? How well are other organizations in the same general business performing? What are the trends in the organization's geographical region?

What has been the history of this organization's negotiations—its objectives, its tactics and strategies, and its successes and failures?

Research

You can practice researching an organization by plugging into one of the many on-line services that act as a gateway to the Internet. By doing so, you can unearth valuable information about your opponent's industry, its current trends, and competitive analyses—which can help you prepare for your negotiations. Several providers are: *America Online, (800) 827-6364; CompuServe Information Service, (800) 848-8199; and reached at Prodigy Services Co., (800) 822-6922.*

TimeSaver

When you enter into the nego-tiation process, make sure you are dealing with an individ-ual who can legitimately assume decision-making power for the organization. Many negotiation cycles end fruitlessly when this commonsense guideline is overlooked.

RED ALERT!

Certain people win their negotiation battles by overpowering their opponents. They do things like:

- Schedule a marathon session to tire and wear you down.
- Insult, intimidate, and berate you to generate irrational anger that will interfere with your reasoning powers.
- Make threats or bluffs to coerce you into accepting less than you may want.

To combat this, call a halt to the proceedings when you get too tired or confused to go on, or have others help you negotiate as a team—round the clock if necessary. Use your intellect to concentrate on the substantive issues, rather than getting personally involved in one-on-one combat across the negotiating table.

Finally, take the other side's statements with a grain of salt. Rely as much on your thorough research into their position as on what they tell you.

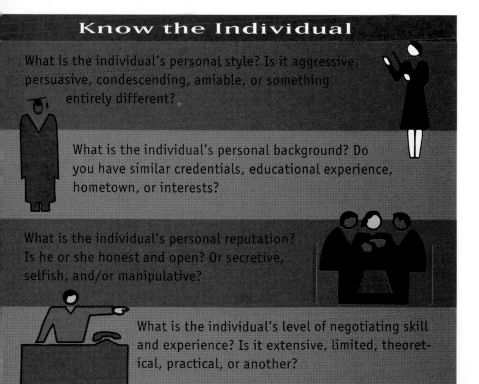

Know the Individual

What is the individual's personal style? Is it aggressive, persuasive, condescending, amiable, or something entirely different?

What is the individual's personal background? Do you have similar credentials, educational experience, hometown, or interests?

What is the individual's personal reputation? Is he or she honest and open? Or secretive, selfish, and/or manipulative?

What is the individual's level of negotiating skill and experience? Is it extensive, limited, theoretical, practical, or another?

RELATED TOPICS

➤ Good Guy/Bad Guy Role-Playing, (pages 74–75)
➤ Bad Temper, (pages 80–81)

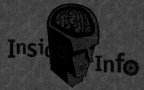

What Is the Context for Negotiations?

Negotiations do not happen in a vacuum. They are influenced by myriad factors—everything from the current economic situation of the negotiating parties to the present and past details of the relationship between them. All of these background issues and influences have a great impact on the course of any negotiation.

When a union and company management have a long and bitter history of conflict, the level of trust and the willingness to compromise are going to be far lower than when they have a history of cooperation. When two strangers meet to negotiate the sale of a car, for example, there's no way they can follow the same process as a father who wants to sell his car to his oldest daughter on terms she can easily meet.

Four Critical Context and Background Factors Are:

1 *The reason for current negotiation.* This could be expiration of a long-term contract, development of a new operating relationship or extension of an existing one to a new project, transfer of property between strangers or family members, or other negotiable issues.

> The clash involves base self-interest and primal greed: the owners want to put a cap on how much players can earn; the players want to defend and expand the right to negotiate salaries they believe they deserve . . . And though the baseball contract officially expired at the end of 1993, [commissioner] Ravitch didn't put the owner's salary-cap proposal on the negotiating table until mid-June.
>
> *Time*, August 22, 1994

> The few bargaining sessions that were held before the strike quickly degenerated into formulaic speeches and sarcastic byplay, all accentuated by the growing animosity between the voluble, chain-smoking Ravitch and the intense, almost humorless Fehr. "Did you see how unpleasant he is?" Ravitch asked rhetorically about Fehr before a joint TV appearance Friday. "It's never been like that in all the negotiations I've been involved in."
>
> *Time*, August 22, 1994

2 *The history between the parties.* In the case of strangers, there may be no previous contact. In other cases, there may be years of working and playing side-by-side.

Understanding the Process

Don't view negotiations as an intellectual exercise in cooperation and harmony. Instead, understand them as a primarily political exercise in relative power, in which certain items and resources are available for distributing (and certain others are not). Negotiations are the process by which the parties allocate to themselves whatever items and resources they can get the other negotiating parties to relinquish.

RED ALERT! Attempt to avoid the arbitration stage of the negotiation process. Simply put, no one wins when an outside party decides your fate. Savvy negotiators abide by this simple fact and bring their flexibility along when sitting down at the bargaining table.

3 *The expectations each party brings to the negotiating table.* These expectations can include ones formed during previous experiences with the other party, as well as expectations based on no real experience—but nevertheless strongly felt. Parties can expect anything from devious behavior to total honesty, from cooperative idealism to cynical selfishness, from crafty maneuvering to naive thinking out loud, and from experimentation in contract terms to reliance on well-tested forms and standards.

What's going on with the game today is confusion, anger and mistrust. The relationship between major league owners and striking players is as acrimonious as ever (negotiations have ceased and aren't scheduled to resume), general managers struggle to figure out the revenue-sharing plan and salary cap implemented by the owners on Dec. 23, and nobody—not owners, G.M.'s, players or fans—knows whether major leaguers or replacement players will suit up on Opening Day.

Newsweek, August 22, 1994

All in all, the 232-day strike cost the owners an estimated $700 million, the players $250 million and the fans 921 regular-season games, not counting the World Series and other postseason games.

Newsweek, August 22, 1994

4 *The external pressures surrounding the negotiation.* Sometimes negotiations are heavily influenced by external business factors, such as the overall trends that are increasing or decreasing the wealth of the negotiating parties. External factors also include the personalities of the negotiators, the time pressure to reach an agreement, and the actions of people who are not parties to the negotiations.

RELATED TOPICS

➤ Know What You Want to Achieve, (pages 6–7)

Inside Info

- Consider your opponent's proposal as an indication of his or her strengths and weaknesses. Your opponent's boldest demands probably reflect areas where he or she feels strongest, while likely glossing over the areas where they feel weakest.

- Use your eyes and ears, as well as research opportunities, to try to keep a running assessment of your opponent's strengths and weaknesses as the negotiations progress. Whenever you can, maneuver the negotiations to capitalize on weaknesses and avoid playing into your opponent's obvious strengths.

Assess Your Opponent's Strengths and Weaknesses

Very few negotiators open important discussions by saying "Just tell me what you want and I'll agree to it" or, conversely, "It's my way or the highway."

In reality, most negotiators are operating from a position somewhere between those two extremes. That's why it's important for you to do your own itemization and assessment of the other party's strengths and weaknesses—regardless of what he or she says or how things initially appear.

Negotiating from Strength

"Negotiating from strength" generally means that one party has more options than its opponent and, thus, cannot be forced into accepting the other side's terms. You can begin to evaluate your opponent's "strengths" by determining how easy or difficult it would be for your opponent to

- get what they want from others if they can't get it from you.
- survive without the products or services received from you.

Other sources of bargaining strength include

- more experience or skill in negotiations.
- access to inside information.
- clearer understanding of desired negotiating goals.

Negotiating from Weakness

"Negotiating from weakness" means that one side of the negotiations has fewer options and may be coerced into agreeing to a less-than-optimal agreement. You can begin to evaluate your opponent's "weaknesses" in terms of how much loss or difficulty your opponent would be likely to incur if

- you refuse to reach an agreement and your opponent must begin new negotiations with another source.
- you decline to meet the timetable for giving the other side what they want.

Other sources of weakness in a bargaining position include

- having to meet a tight deadline that can't be extended.
- lack of vision about what is ultimately important and what's not.
- unwillingness to take fair risks to reach negotiating goals.

CASE IN POINT

You're negotiating with Technos Corporation on behalf of Cosmocom. You feel that Technos can't easily go anywhere else to get what they want, and without it their business would drop off substantially. Because of this, Technos desperately needs to get supplies coming in again within thirty days.

However, the negotiator for Technos is a lot more skilled than you are, and appears to have detailed information on Cosmocom's costs of production.

To play into Technos's weaknesses, you might drag your feet as a stall tactic to increase the pressure of their thirty-day deadline.

To limit the advantage of Technos's inside information, you develop and bring up cost figures that express another accounting point of view—contradicting the information Technos has acquired.

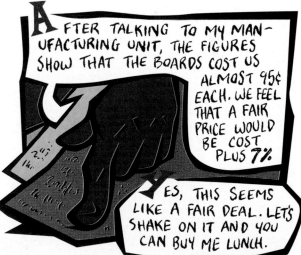

RED ALERT! Be careful not to jump too quickly to agree to any terms—even if you think you understand them—so your opponent's skill and expertise count for less.

RELATED TOPICS

➤ Making the Most of a Weak Position (pages 7–8)

➤ After You, I Insist. . ., (pages 50–51)

Trade One Concession for Another

As negotiations proceed, keep track of the concessions you're willing to make, without openly agreeing to any of them. Then, as you press the other side for agreement to a concession you want, offer one of your appropriate prepared concessions as a "quid pro quo."

Keep asking for concessions in the form of "If I agree to this, will you agree to that?"

In an ideal world, you enter a negotiating room, receive everything you want, agree to everything the other side wants, and leave the room a very happy person.

But in the real world of practical negotiations, you'll nearly always be forced to agree to terms you'd rather not, and find yourself fighting hard to obtain the terms you feel are only necessary, minimally fair, and appropriate.

That's why the most successful negotiators have developed a rhythm of "give one, get one" to which they strictly adhere.

The idea is never to simply agree to a request from the other side. Instead, couch all your responses to their offers in terms of a trade. This way, you're expressing your willingness to compromise without offering the other side any gifts.

RED ALERT!

One of the tricks negotiators like to use on the unwary is to discuss two related points as if they will be agreed on simultaneously, then suddenly dump the second one as soon as they get your agreement to the first.

For example, you may be discussing your willingness to pay a higher wage in return for your employees' willingness to accept a longer workday. After a while, both sides help draft one plan for higher wages, plus a separate plan for implementing a new schedule. You sign the wage plan only to discover that the other side wants to delay signing the related agreement.

To protect yourself from such sandbagging, make no statements about "final" agreements on any *one* issue until you've reached agreement on *all* the issues.

Don't use phrases like:

"Yes."

"I don't see why not."

"I agree to that."

Instead, use phrases like:

"We will accept your terms if you'll accept our terms."

"If I agree to this, will you agree to that?"

"That seems acceptable for now."

CASE IN POINT

A debtor and creditor recently went to small claims court to settle their differences. But before their case could be heard by the judge, a professional mediator enticed them both into a negotiation session.

There, the debtor argued persuasively that the creditor was asking for too high a repayment, whereupon the mediator turned to the creditor and asked: "Will you agree to reduce the amount from $5,000 to $4,000?"

A less skillful negotiator might have said, "Yes," and then begun negotiating on a separate issue. But this negotiator, wise in the ways of debtors, instead replied, "If I agree to that, will you agree to start making payments immediately?"

This "give one, get one" approach worked here as a perfect technique to avoid making a one-way concession that might not be repaid in kind by the other party.

$5,000!

$4,000?

MAYBE

YES

NO

RELATED TOPICS

➤ Small Concessions Can Make You a Winner, (pages 52–53)

OCTOBER

S	M	T	W	T	F	S
..	..	1	2	3	4	5
6	7	8	9	10	11	12
13	14	15	16	17	18	19
20	21	22	23	24	25	26
27	28	29	30	31	..	..

Communicate Clearly

Make sure everyone understands you.

Take accurate notes and refer to them often.

Negotiations depend on clear communications as much as enjoyment of the Grand Canyon depends on good visibility. Without it, there's not much chance of having a meaningful experience.

Communications during negotiation is necessarily a two-way street. That is, it's just as important to make sure you understand the other party as it is to make sure the other party understands you.

The reasons for this are simple:

Intentionally misunderstanding you, or misleading you, is one way some negotiators try to gain an advantage, create confusion, or win concessions they couldn't obtain through other methods.

Unintentional misunderstandings often become time bombs that explode at unexpected moments, often toward the end of difficult negotiations. People suddenly realize they don't agree on an item they thought they'd finished, and the resulting disappointment or dismay tends to destroy much of the progress toward agreement that has already been achieved on other issues.

That's why you should be careful as you move from point to point in a negotiation. As necessary, use any or all of the tips included here to keep communications between the parties crystal clear.

Keeping Communication Clear

Be explicit about:

• What point you're presently discussing.

• Each offer you make to the other side.

• What objections your side has to a given offer.

• What changes will facilitate agreement on the current point.

• What terms you think you're agreeing to.

• When you move from discussion of one point to another.

Watch out for the negotiating opponent who too quickly accepts a compromise on a point that has previously been the subject of much dissension. He may be intentionally—or unintentionally—misunderstanding what compromise you've proposed.

If you suspect you've been misunderstood on a point of any significance, stop the conversation, return to that topic, and go over it again. If necessary, put the compromise in writing and have the other party initial it.

Communicating

One of the most difficult aspects of maintaining clear communications is to say *exactly* what you mean. It's too easy—and very common—to "shoot from the hip" by speaking before you've given an issue, offer, suggestion, or comment from the other side sufficient time and thought.

To combat this, practice a judicious pause. Use it in two ways:

1 Use it while you're speaking. During a complicated thought or when expressing a subtle nuance, don't speak the first word that comes to mind. Instead, pause for a moment and see if you can find a better, more accurate word to use in its place.

2 Use it once you've finished listening to someone else speak, and you're ready to begin your own utterance. Don't speak immediately. Instead, wait a heartbeat or two, a breath or two, or even longer.

RELATED TOPICS

➤ **Make Sure the Other Side Hears You,** (pages 30–31)

➤ **Control Your Side's Communication,** (pages 32–33)

Before you respond to your opponent, pause for a moment to reflect on what has been said. By taking this brief instant to fully consider his or her statements, you can better plan your response in order to appeal to your opponent's goals and objectives.

Gain the Value of Intelligent Listening

WORDS TO LIVE BY

"So when you are listening to somebody, completely, attentively, then you are listening not only to the words, but also to the feeling of what is being conveyed, to the whole of it, not part of it."
—Jiddu Krishnamurti

At any moment in any conversation, there are two processes: the speaking process and the listening process. Unfortunately, in ordinary conversations most people simply wait their turn to speak again instead of actively listening.

But in negotiations, you can't afford to miss a single nuance, implication, or inference of what the other side communicates. If you do, you may easily ignore vital information, strong clues to a weakness in the other party's negotiating position, or even signals about how you can more easily get what you want.

> To glean every bit of important information from the other side, you must listen hard, closely, continuously, and intelligently.

Listening

You can get more from intelligent listening by making the other side a better talker. To do this, make a lot of eye contact, smile and nod in empathy with the other side's major points, and behave as though you find their arguments persuasive.

This will tend to draw out the other side, giving them the feeling you're easier to negotiate with, and handing you more information to analyze for a better understanding of your opponent.

Intelligent Listening

1 Take Notes

Not only is it difficult to remember everything the other party to a negotiation is telling you, but it's difficult to put all the points, arguments, and background information together into a clear picture of where the other side is coming from, and what they want. By taking notes, you give yourself a chance to make better sense of all the remarks the other party makes. You also forget less, and can go back through your notes to find inconsistencies or details that will help you reach the agreement you want.

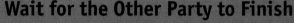

TimeSaver
As you listen, don't limit your focus on just points of disagreement. Note areas where both sides agree, as well. This helps eliminate a lot of unnecessary discussion and frees up more time and energy for negotiation on the issues that remain in contention.

2 Pay Close Attention

Maintain a high level of alertness, and focus single-mindedly on what the other side is communicating. Listen to their words. Watch their body language. Analyze the thinking that lies underneath what they're telling you.

Don't talk strategy with others on your team. Don't plan your rebuttal. Don't count your winnings or contemplate your losses in the negotiations to come. If you feel your attention slipping, try to call a halt while you refresh yourself.

3 Wait for the Other Party to Finish

One of the biggest mistakes a negotiator can make is to be too eager to respond or to initiate the next exchange of ideas. There's great value in letting the other talk and talk and talk until they run down and stop by themselves.

First, it's easy for the other side to prepare remarks—in writing or through brief mental rehearsals—that carefully cover its weaknesses and convey an impression they want you to receive. But when they come to the end of their prepared remarks, they may well begin to improvise additional comments that reveal a great deal more to the intelligent listener.

Second, as the other side begins to repeat earlier comments, offer increasingly weaker arguments in favor of its position, and generally ramble on too long, it gives you extra time to analyze what they've said and understand it in all its nuances. For example, your first reaction to an offer might be to accept it. But a second thought, which you wouldn't experience if you didn't devote extra time to intelligent listening, might be that the proposal contains a new problem that would make the present situation even worse.

RELATED TOPICS

➤ Ask All the Key Questions, (pages 26–27)

Ask All the Key Questions

When negotiations begin, all parties come to the table with information, and with questions for and about those across the table. Of course, you can and should find your own answers to some of these questions. But sometimes you really must ask. When you do, be sure to:

1. *Avoid any kind of adversarial tone.* You're not a lawyer cross-examining a lying witness. You're a sweet-tempered negotiator trying to advance toward a deal that's fair and beneficial for all parties involved. So keep your voice friendly, your attitude cooperative and respectful, and your body language open and nonthreatening.

2. *Be persistent.* Many times, questions honestly do get lost in the conversations that ensue. Other times, however, your negotiating opponent tries to sidestep tough questions by ignoring them. Keep coming back to questions that will get you the answers you want and need.

You will always want answers to the following questions:

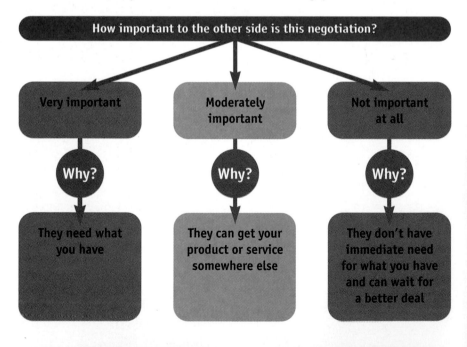

Getting Answers

Don't let an unanswered question escape you. It's not uncommon for you to ask a question and get the answer: "Gee, I don't know. But I'll find out and get back to you."

Follow up on these unanswered questions. If the information was important enough to ask about, it's important enough to discover the answer. A more crucial reason is that the other side may not want to give up the answer so readily. They'll "forget" to get back to you, and they'll hope you'll let it "slide" as well.

If you do let it slide, and you miss out on some important information, you have no one but yourself to blame.

RED ALERT! Be sure to separate opinion and vague promises from hard facts. If you ask about delivery dates, for example, don't be satisfied when the other side says: "There's no problem. I'm sure we can agree on a delivery date that'll be satisfactory to you." That's only an opinion, and it should carry far less weight than when the other side says: "We can deliver what you want by the thirty-first," or the even more revealing, "We'll meet any delivery date you specify."

What external factors—business cycles, competition, industry changes, etc.—are pressuring each side both toward and away from reaching an agreement?

- Economic recession
- Industry slowdown
- New competitor in marketplace

What has been the history of negotiations—objectives, tactics, strategies, and success—with the other side?

- Opponent comes to the table willing to negotiate
  - Reach agreement
- Past difficulties with your organization make your opponent wary of you
  - Negotiations strained, break down
  - You win over opponent, enter into equitable negotiations

RELATED TOPICS

➤ What is the Context for Negotiations?, (pages 16–17)

Inside Info

A *persuasive* argument should not be interpreted as an *aggressive* argument. If your opponent feels pushed or intimidated, he or she will be less likely to give you what you want.

WORDS TO
LIVE BY

"Testimony is like an arrow shot from a long-bow; its force depends on the strength of the hand that draws it. But argument is like an arrow from a cross-bow, which has equal force if drawn by a child or a man."

—Charles Boyle

Make Your Arguments Persuasive

Most negotiations are a lot more complex than winning an argument over a bit of television trivia. But many times the process is essentially the same: It's your job as negotiator to put forward persuasive arguments that will convince the other side to agree with and give you what you want.

So it's important to strengthen the negotiating tactics you'll use to make your arguments as persuasive as possible. Here are some basic rules to help you:

1 Assertions of fact are often useful. But you'll persuade more people when you back up your assertions with books, photos, "white papers," reports, even newspaper articles that confirm the same thing.

2 Try to understand the details and factors central to the negotiation. But you'll gain more respect and cooperation from the other side if you bring in experts to make key arguments for you.

RED ALERT!

It is possible to over-document, oversupport, and overemphasize the "hot buttons" associated with one particular argument. Whether or not you are doing so is one of the most difficult calls for a negotiator to make. You don't want to back off too soon, but neither do you want to fall short of persuading the other side that your own argument should be the controlling factor in whatever agreement you reach.

Be ready to back off, therefore, when you sense that the other side has reached its limit of interest, tolerance, and movement in the direction you want them to go.

"We need to strike while the iron is hot."

"Six of one and half dozen of the other."

"Let's make no bones about this deal."

"I'll carry the ball here."

"Time is money."

3 Colorful words and apt metaphors certainly increase interest level and aid understanding. But you'll persuade fewer people if you try to drag them too far, too fast, with hyperbole and overstatement they recognize as hogwash. In general, it's better to understate a powerful argument than to overstate a weak one.

4 The other side is watching. So the more you try to ignore and cover up the obvious weaknesses of your position, the more glaring they will appear. It's foolish and often counterpersuasive to assert that your obvious weaknesses are not really weak. The more persuasive tactic is simply to be open about weaknesses, but downplay their overall importance in comparison with other factors where your position happens to be very strong.

RELATED TOPICS

➤ The Art of Persuasion, (pages 68–69)

➤ Splitting the Difference, (pages 88–89)

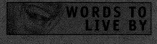

Make Sure the Other Side Hears You

Just as your level of alertness can fade and your interest wane during part of the proceedings because you're concentrating on something that seems more important at the moment, the same can occur to those across from you at the negotiating table.

But you don't want to be ignored, relegated to the background, or be the target of "gamesmanship." In short, when you're making a presentation, you want it to be heard.

Here are some ways to gain the other side's attention whenever you want to be sure they pay close attention to what you're saying:

Raise Your Voice

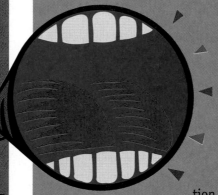

Shouting is an immature, ineffective way to make your points, but it certainly gets people's attention. You don't want to shout too often, or for too many seconds at a time. But once in a while, a foghorn voice calling out "I'm talking about profits, here, ladies and gentlemen!", or some such remark, will go a long way toward getting your words the attention they deserve.

Lower Your Voice

Actors with limited talent often shift to a whispering voice as a way to show emotions they can't otherwise act out. There's something about a very soft voice that—at the right times and in the right circumstances—commands more attention than the loudest vocal cry.

One technique is simply to talk in a softer-than-normal voice. You might want to practice gradually lowering your volume, so that for a few minutes or more others must sit quietly and cock one ear toward you to catch all your words.

CASE IN POINT

Many of the greatest speakers in history—from Frederick Douglass to John F. Kennedy—have utilized strong personal points to influence their audiences. By directing your pitch to an area your opponent will be most responsive to, you stand a greater chance of persuading the other side to meet your terms.

If you're negotiating for a lower purchase price from your opponent, for example, you may want to put it in terms of overall quantity. You can do this easily by simply saying, "I'd like to purchase many units from you over the long run, but I just can't commit to your price."

If your opponent wants your long-term business, he or she will find a way to compromise to meet your terms.

SITUATION

Negotiating for Lower Purchase Price

OFFER

Will Price Be Adjusted for Long-Term Order?

COMPROMISE

Opponent Chooses Long-Term Over Short-Term Interests

Touch on the Hottest Topic

During protracted negotiations, it's impossible for everyone to maintain full alertness all the time. You can snap them to attention, however, with a verbal cracking of the whip. All you must do is somehow weave into your presentation or discussion a sentence or two about the single most important topic in these ongoing negotiations.

Put on a Demonstration

Just like a picture, a demonstration is very often worth a thousand words. To get more attention for your ideas and arguments, practice putting them in vivid, visual terms that you can act out, demonstrate, or otherwise illustrate when those across the table starting putting their heads in their hands. Start collecting interesting props, noise-makers, ideas for surprising situations, and other potential attention-getters. Try to prepare at least one for each negotiation in which you participate.

➤ **Make Your Arguments Most Persuasive, (pages 28–29)**

Inside Info

Bring a trusted friend to at least the first negotiating session—not to participate, but to observe. Ask him or her to watch for any signs that others on your team are out of sync with your main strategy and message to those across the negotiating table.

He or she can signal you immediately upon spotting any potential problems, so you can cut the meeting short and herd your own team into line before you attempt to negotiate again.

Control Your Side's Communication

I f you're negotiating alone against another party, there's no one else on your side to leak your position, undermine your authority, or make any statement that might counter what you're trying to achieve.

But as you become a more seasoned and skillful negotiator, it's more and more likely you'll be part of a negotiating team—even if it's only you and your spouse—fighting for higher stakes—to secure a better price on your next home.

So it's important to understand the concepts that underlie team negotiations, particularly those concepts that help you keep the team from cutting its own throat by communicating the wrong message to people on the other side.

The main factors in controlling your side's communication include:

Developing team loyalty

Developing team consensus

WORDS TO LIVE BY

"Talk to a man about himself and he will listen for hours."
—Benjamin Disraeli

Training team members in basic communications skills

TimeSaver
Much like football or basketball games, many negotiating sessions today are video- or audiotaped to be reviewed after the fact. By doing so, players are more self-conscious of their behavior and are less likely to make blatant errors in communication.

Pssst!

RED ALERT! In highly confidential negotiations, be careful about who joins your negotiating team. Some individuals have personal agendas they are acting on—from job searching to downright sabotage—and can leak valuable information that can potentially undermine your success.

Many people compromise the privacy of negotiating positions and background information because they're disgruntled or resentful of intra-team politics. Prevent such problems by having a designated **"team manager"** who concentrates on building each person's loyalty to the overall goals of the negotiating team.

Dissension within the ranks is a prime source of unauthorized communication to the other side—whether it's a photocopy of a vital position paper or body language that conveys "Don't think we all agree with what he's saying."

But dissension nearly always disappears when the team manager tries to **involve all the team members** in setting negotiating goals, making decisions, and playing a useful role in the negotiation process.

Many negotiating team members have no idea how much inside information the other side can glean from a wink, a stare, an embarrassed smile, or urgent scribbling from among the team members who aren't speaking out loud.

That's why a small investment in **communications training** will help the group keep a tighter grip on the information and attitudes they'd rather the other side does not discover, or even suspect.

RELATED TOPICS

➤ "Worst-Case" Scenarios, (pages 54–55)

The Power of Deadlines

Inside Info

While you should generally behave as though deadlines are always extremely important, keep in mind that deadlines the other side imposes may also be a powerful negotiating tool to force your hand.

By understanding this, you can keep negotiating at a steady pace—maintaining a clear vision of your goals. Meanwhile, "use the clock" to your advantage by taking longer to deliberate, longer to formulate responses, and longer to research a matter or "get the facts" from an expert.

Ever notice how athletes and team owners, or unions and management can't seem to agree on anything in the early stages of a contract negotiation? But as the date for a strike or a lockout looms closer, suddenly they find ways to resolve complex issues that would ordinarily have stumped King Solomon.

That's the power of deadlines.

The presence of a firm deadline that you've imposed on the proceedings immediately puts the people across the negotiating table at a disadvantage. Their options become more limited. They feel the pressure of time. They begin to wonder what other sources they can find for the things you presently want from them.

Just as deadlines can be a powerful ally, the other side can use them as an equally powerful enemy of your cause. Be aware of deadlines the other side proposes and their implications if you choose to let these deadlines expire. If you sense the other side is using the deadline as one more weapon to force you into an unfair agreement, be ready to counterattack with an earlier deadline of your own.

You can harness deadlines in many different ways to benefit your side in the negotiation.

Set a Deadline

The easiest way to get deadline power on your side is to set one yourself. "Unless we can agree by July 21st," you can intone dramatically, "we'll look elsewhere for a deal." A simple way to enforce this is to let your opponent know you'll be unavailable after the date you've established—whether you have other commitments or are beginning a new project.

Find a Deadline

Many deadlines exist naturally—a traditional start-up or cut-off date for such things as the debut of new-model cars, shopping for Christmas, or celebrating Mother's Day—and good negotiators know where to find them. Fixed deadlines, such as upcoming trade shows or conventions, or seasonal weather changes that make construction projects or baseball games more difficult, gain the power of deadlines without having to play the bad guy who establishes an artificial one.

Ask for a Deadline

Suppose you're representing emergency room nurses who can't get the local hospital to renew their contract. You can create a lot of pressure in your favor by asking publicly: "Exactly how long do you think we should be willing to work without a contract?"

Or, if you're subscribing to a cable TV company that delivers crummy reception, why not ask the cable operator (in writing): "How long do you think I should continue to pay for this unsatisfactory service you're giving me?"

When the other side names a date, you've got a deadline working for you.

Defy a Deadline

In extreme circumstances, you can purposely let a deadline expire. Normally, you'd be in the wrong. But if the other side refuses to make a fair offer, you can successfully use the attention to argue your case in a wider forum.

RELATED TOPICS

➤ Stonewalling, (pages 76–77)

➤ Take It or Leave It, (pages 84–85)

➤ It's OK to Walk, (pages 86–87)

Keep Your Expectations Reasonable

I get everything; you get nothing. I pay nothing; you pay everything. I have all the rights and options; you have none. I'm liable for nothing that goes wrong; you're liable for everything. I can keep this contract going forever; you can never get out of it."

That's the classic summary of the contracts many people offer others to accept and sign.

Of course, only a few contracts are actually written this way, but this type of thinking is totally at odds with the kind of win-win negotiations that more and more people are conducting these days. Today, the classic contract can be summed up in four simple words:

"We share everything fairly."

That's why keeping your expectations reasonable is critically important—at least while you're still trying to conduct win-win negotiations. Nothing will undermine a win-win mood faster than wading into battle with a fistful of unreasonable expectations.

X
SIGNATURE:

RED ALERT!

Don't be a sucker. Go into a negotiation with a win-win attitude, sure. But if you see the other party light up a big fat cigar and stick his feet up on the table while fighting like hell for all the things he wants, it would be foolish for you to give his concerns and well-being as much weight as you give your own.

Money

Everyone wants a fair share. It's unreasonable to expect that one party to the negotiations will be happy with less money than the others.

The guiding principles here should be that everyone gets rewarded in direct proportion to the value of their contribution, and the amount of risk they accept in making that contribution.

Power

Don't expect that some people will give up a fair share of control over a project, a relationship, a company, or anything else. Sure, some people aren't interested in being the leader. But they're not interested in being the slave, either.

Instead, go for the modern paradigm: Everyone has some influence over the final product, the final design, the final decision.

Options

In this rapidly changing world it's unreasonable to expect that people will agree to conditions that will lock them into a fixed situation. Everyone wants a chance to be flexible when conditions change.

So don't bargain for absolute certainty in places where you don't need it. Agree to more flexible wording like "reasonable," "usual," "normal," "in most cases," and so forth.

Rights and Responsibilities

They go hand in hand. Don't expect people to accept responsibilities for things that can go wrong without the authority or the right to make things come out right.

That's why a reasonable expectation is spread rights and responsibilities like oil and vinegar on a salad—evenly, and not too much for any one person.

Ownership

It's unreasonable to expect that people will contribute to the success of any enterprise without having some "ownership," in the broadest possible sense of the word.

This ownership is an equity of ideas, a profit for intellectual labor. Today, people want ownership of their politics, their schools, their beliefs, and their communities, as well as their work. You want to support ownership too, because without ownership individuals have little or no interest in the success of your negotiations.

TimeSaver
Ask the other party, right up front, what they want. It's far faster to ask and answer this question than to play a cat-and-mouse guessing game. If you're both interested in a win-win solution, you'll save a lot of time by exchanging wish lists and seeing how many of the other side's wishes each of you can satisfy.

RELATED TOPICS

➤ Creative Problem Solving, (pages 60–61)

➤ The Art of Conciliation, (pages 64–65)

Inside Info

Rank your expectations in order of importance, so you spend more time and energy negotiating for what you want the most.

Get What You Really Want

In negotiations, as in life, expectations play a big role in determining what you get. Imagine two people, each negotiating separately with a third person to buy a new car. One person wants to get a decent set of wheels at a price she can afford. That's what she comes away with. The second person wants the absolutely top-of-the-line model, but he doesn't want to pay much more for all the extras.

Which one do you think is likely to drive the harder bargain—and the nicer car—at a bargain price?

Of course, just wanting to acquire the sun, the moon, and the stars through negotiation does not guarantee you will get them. But asking for only one or two does guarantee you won't get all three.

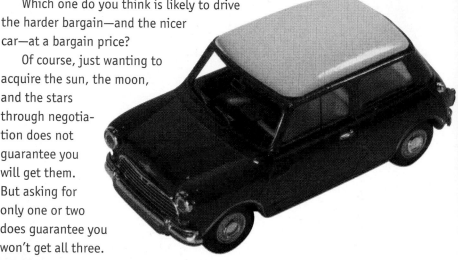

RED ALERT!

Although wanting more is better than wanting less from a negotiation, there is a limit. If you expect and ask for too much, you'll just anger the people on the other side. You could even destroy any chance for an agreement. Remember the win-win approach and be sure your expectations and demands remain reasonable to all parties.

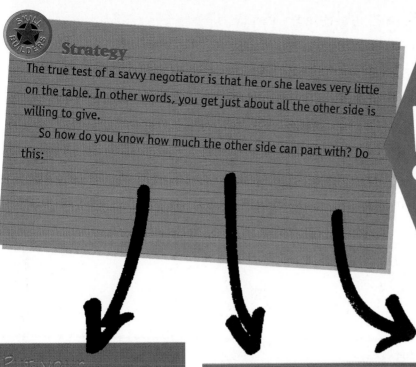

Strategy

The true test of a savvy negotiator is that he or she leaves very little on the table. In other words, you get just about all the other side is willing to give.

So how do you know how much the other side can part with? Do this:

By going through this exercise for every negotiation, you'll build up your ability to assess how much you can obtain from the other party, and make yourself a more skillful, successful negotiator with every bargaining experience you gather.

Put your negotiation in context:

Do some research among colleagues, in libraries, and on the Internet to determine what other parties in similar discussions have agreed to most recently.

Make adjustments:

Evaluate the differences between those comparable negotiations and yours. Was the other party bigger or smaller? Richer or poorer? Facing better or worse prospects for the future? Ask the same questions for the party on the same side of the table as you.

Role-play:

Put yourself in your negotiating opponent's shoes. What's important? What concessions can you comfortably make?

CASE IN POINT

Scott Electronics was looking to expand their office space and found the perfect place—Infinity Office Park. Although the Infinity Park was 80 percent leased, Scott decided to offer only 85¢ a square foot, when the going lease price was over $2.00. Infinity was so incensed by Scott's offer that they wouldn't entertain a counteroffer, even though Scott would have been willing to pay the full rate.

At the same time, Congress Electronics wanted the same space and offered the Infinity Management $1.65 a square foot with several months free rent over the lease period included. The office park quickly came to an agreement with Congress, because they had made a good faith offer for the space.

RELATED TOPICS

➤ Small Concessions Can Make You a Winner, (pages 52–53)

➤ Stay Focused on Your Goals, (pages 58–59)

Timing Is Everything!

The art of timing negotiations to your best advantage often spells the difference between success—getting what you want from the other party—and failure—getting less than you want, or nothing at all.

Like waves on a beach, the timing of any negotiation is subject to many influences, which all interact, although any one of them can suddenly become the dominant force. These influences include:

Seasonal Changes

The fashion and automobile industries are prime examples of ongoing concerns that have definite high and low points throughout the year. You can probably think of a dozen others. If you're negotiating with an organization or an individual influenced (whether emotionally, financially, or any other way) by the seasons, it's important to select the right season for negotiations.

Business Cycles

Although most businesses weather the same regular periods of relatively good and bad times, response to negotiations can be dramatically different. When the business cycle is going well, the other side may have more to share with you. Some may be empowered by this positive cycle and thus less inclined to work with you, while others will enthusiastically share their resources. Near the bottom of the business cycle, your negotiating opponent may be more humble and cooperative but may also have less to bargain with.

Portland WEEK

$1 Single Copy/3

VOLUME 12, NUMBER 3

TriQuint joining chip plant boom

Stock offer paves way for Portland expansion

By STEVE LAW

Homegrown TriQuint Semiconductor Inc. hopes to join the crowd of new chip plants by building a factory and headquarters at Hillsboro's Dawson Creek

Dawson Creek awash in growth

The TriQuint deal is one of a

Circumstances

An individual or organization with bad luck or poor management skills may falter even at the top of a business cycle that coincides with their usual busy season. Consider the specific fortunes of your negotiating opponent as you try to time your negotiations to your best advantage.

Biorhythms

There may be little or no scientific basis for the theory of biorhythms, but no one denies that every individual experiences better and worse days, weeks, or months.

If you negotiate with your opponent on a bad day, will you fare better than if you catch him or her on a good day?

Momentum

On a given day, almost any decent negotiator can win important compromises from almost any other negotiator. The "momentum" factor is an nonscientific appraisal that sums up how well you're performing in comparison to your opposite number. When you've got the momentum on your side, go for the big one. When you've lost the momentum, try to limit your losses.

Timing

The most difficult part of timing your negotiations is to align each step of the process with the appropriate time in the other person's cycle to give your side the biggest advantage. Consider carefully when it might be best to:

Start your negotiations
when momentum can most easily be gathered or lost.

Conduct the midsection of your negotiations when
many thorny issues are resolved. Rising or high portions of the cycle are least damaging to you here.

Wind up your negotiations
when the most difficult issues are often discussed, and when one side or the other can run out of gas and capitulate to the other side's demands. Catching your negotiating opponent at a low point may give you a decided advantage.

RELATED TOPICS

➤ Know When It's Time to Quit, (pages 72–73)

Making a Fair Deal

In the classic Westerns, the bad guys would often waylay a man traveling alone across the desert. They'd take his horse, his gun, and his money. But they'd leave him his boots, his long johns, and some water.

Why? Because taking any of these would amount to murder.

It's much the same in negotiations. You can bargain as hard as you want, but if you take too much, you'll be stepping over the line. This may not amount to murder, literally, but taking too much will make the other side more reluc-tant—and less able—to strike another bargain with you later on.

Because of your win-win attitude toward negotiations, you'll want to se-cure for your own side a fair share of what's on the table. But you'll want to leave enough for the other side to be happy, too.

If someone seems out to fleece you completely, consider making no deal at all. Their attitude should be interpreted as a bold, flashing neon sign that reads: "I'm not here for the long haul. I don't want to maintain a relationship with you, and I won't stay around to make an-other deal with you when this one runs out."

Process

A good procedure to follow before you enter into any negotiation is this:

1. Create a wish list that includes everything you'd like to obtain from this negotiation.
2. Review the wish list to see what the other side can reasonably deliver, and what is way out of bounds.
3. Temper your reasonable demands or expectations down to a level you feel the other party can meet.

CASE IN POINT

One way to leave enough for the other side is to temper your side's demands. For example, two designers were partners in a company that received an unexpected $10,000 tax rebate last year. In their discussions about what to do with the money, one partner wanted to reinvest it all. The other partner wanted to split the rebate and take it as a bonus compensation for her recent long work hours. Both options would have been mutually beneficial, yet each would have felt short-changed.

As an alternative, both women argued for a win-win resolution to the dispute. In the end, each partner got $5,000 from the tax rebate check, each reinvested half, and both felt very satisfied.

$10,000 Tax Rebate

SITUATION

Two Partners

DILEMMA

| Reinvest | Bonus |

RESOLUTION

**Each Reinvested 1/2
Each Spent 1/2**

RELATED TOPICS

➤ Splitting the Difference, (pages 88–89)

Inside Info

Use the home court advantage not only to sell your ideas but also your company. A brilliantly staged presentation aided by competent support staff shows your opponent that your business is well run and is a good opportunity for negotiation.

Use Your Home Court Advantage

When you're holding negotiations in your own offices, or at least in your hometown, the advantages you gain from not traveling to a distant negotiation site are immense in terms of your position as opposed to that of your opponent. These advantages include:

1 Sleep
Because you're sleeping at home and your internal clock is uninterrupted, you're more rested and comfortable.

2 Available Resources
Because you're on your own turf and have all your usual resources readily available, you can respond more swiftly to sudden changes in the direction of the negotiation. You'll then be prepared to answer sudden inquiries with more complete data, and back up your own proposals with better-prepared presentations.

3 Comfortable Pace
Because you may have less need to finish within certain time constraints, you can approach the negotiations at your own pace and take the time to win the concessions you want.

4 Bargaining Incentive
Because the other side has traveled so far, they may be less inclined to leave the negotiations without an agreement or to pull out all together. They have a far stronger incentive than you to continue talking when both sides are so geographically distant.

WORDS TO LIVE BY

"There's no place like home."

—Judy Garland,
The Wizard of Oz

Hospitality

Negotiations will start off on a better footing if the other side has received the "red carpet" treatment. Offer to do everything from making reservations (and consider paying for their stay) in a quality hotel that offers business services to providing limousines for every inch of ground transportation.

The other side may get the home court advantage when negotiations are scheduled at their site. Take care to ensure that the logistical tables don't turn against you. Get plenty of rest—avoiding red-eye flights—and arrive early to the presentation so you'll be able to set up and clear your head before the meetings begin. Stay in close contact with your home office, and keep focused on the immediate goals of your negotiations.

CASE IN POINT

Your company is trying to sell a potential client on a new industrial part your R&D team has developed. You invite them to your headquarters for the talks, which allows you to have your full staff on hand for any possible crisis or change that could occur. In the end, this on-the-spot flexibility enables you to close the deal in one day.

The morning begins with a presentation of design samples by the R&D team

MORNING

Prospective client requests changes to samples

The R&D team hurries to their studio and make modifications to the samples based on input from the meeting

The meeting turns to discussions about marketing strategies

LUNCH

Budget discussions start, then are tabled

The R&D team presents revised design samples. Client accepts revisions, and prototype development begins

RELATED TOPICS

➤ **Control the Conference Setting, (pages 56–57)**

Inside Info

Although the telephone is a valuable tool in negotiations, you must be able to determine when it is best to meet in person. This could include making a presentation of visual images such as financial projection charts or art for an album cover.

If you've never made personal contact with your opponent, you may choose to begin your negotiations in person and then continue by telephone. Or, if you've come to an agreement on a large, long-term negotiation, both sides may elect to meet for signature of the final papers and a friendly handshake.

WORDS TO LIVE BY

"Grammar and logic free language from being at the mercy of the tone of voice."
—Rosenstock-Huessy

Negotiating by Telephone

It can be difficult to conduct a round of serious negotiations by telephone, but often it's the only option. Although certain conversational elements we've come to count on—such as body language—are lost, convenience and immediacy can take their place, making the telephone a highly desirable way of doing business for busy negotiators.

A telephone conversation is generally considered less formal than a letter, and can be used to create an atmosphere of cooperation. As such, a telephone can be a good means of testing the waters, making an emotional appeal, pitching a controversial idea, or persuading someone to try something new.

Although the same rules of etiquette apply to both telephone and face-to-face negotiations, not everyone observes them. Many of your opponents may believe that when an impasse is reached, it's far easier to hang up the telephone than to work it out. On the other hand, it's also easier to pick up where negotiations left off, since the costly element of travel doesn't come into play.

As the world of technology expands, more and more negotiations will take place with the help of fiber optic wires. **Learning to use these tools** to the best advantage gives you a decided edge in any negotiation.

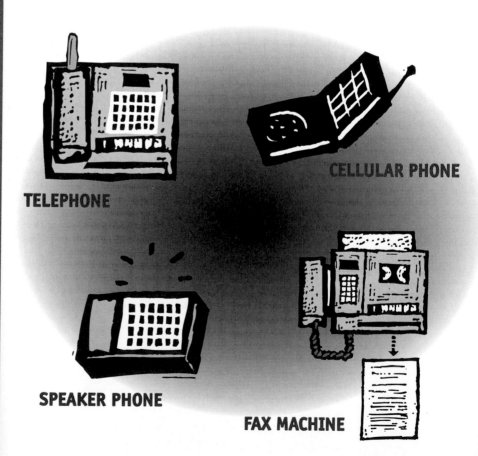

TELEPHONE

CELLULAR PHONE

SPEAKER PHONE

FAX MACHINE

Telephones today are simply not secure. If you're discussing important financial or personal matters over the telephone—particularly over a cellular telephone—you can't be sure someone isn't listening in.

If your negotiations involve security- or time-sensitive information, using the telephone may not be your best choice. If you need to use the telephone, you can make the conversation less revealing by using code phrases such as "the time frame you outlined," "where we met last time," even "the project," for concepts only you and the other party can understand.

TimeSaver
Telephones are great timesavers in negotiations. Use them to:
- Replace routine meetings.
- Fax documents for review, revisions, or approval.
- Make preliminary offers or float trial ideas.

Preparation

Talking on the telephone seems like an imitation of talking face-to-face. But's it not. You may say the same words, but they suddenly have a different meaning since you can't back up your words with gestures, smiles, or body language. Here are some steps to improve telephone communication:

1. Take notes
2. Ask for help
3. Get interrupted
4. Hang up

1 Write down what you want to say beforehand, and work from your notes as you speak.

2 Have others on your team listen in occasionally, or use a speakerphone, and get their input on your presentation, the responses, and your overall manner with the other side.

3 People are so used to "call waiting" and "the other line is ringing" that you can stage as many interruptions in a conversation as you need. Use this, however, only when you need a minute to pull your thoughts together—not as a regular device.

4 Once the other side has had its say, you can easily end a telephone conversation by saying "Well, that's an interesting point. Let me think about it and call you tomorrow." It would be far less convenient to try the same tactic in a face-to-face meeting.

RELATED TOPICS

➤ Communicate Clearly, (pages 22–23)

Make Sure the Other Side Hears You, (pages 30–31)

Inside Info

Although the world of negotiations has room for successful negotiators with many different styles, your own particular style may not appeal to every client. Be aware when your personal approach is not being received well or is losing points for your side. It may be time to rethink your style and retool your approach.

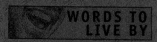

WORDS TO LIVE BY

"One essential to success is that your desire be an all-obsessing one, your thoughts and aims be coordinated, and your energy be concentrated and applied without letup."

—Claude M. Bristol

What's Your Negotiating Style?

People with limited negotiation experience tend to think that top-flight negotiators are either bullies or sorcerers: They either overpower those across the table or somehow magically convince them into accepting less than they want.

But this isn't true. As a talented negotiator you must understand the strengths and weaknesses of individual personalities. Then, you learn to make the best of your strengths while protecting yourself in the areas where you're aware that you're weak.

Consider your track record, and ask your peers and colleagues for clues to your native style. For example, are you:

Persuasive?

Whether it's through native charm or the ability to weave dream-pictures that others buy into, you've always been able to convince people to go along with your point of view. Concentrate on face-to-face discussions at a strategic level, gain agreements in principle, and leave the details for later or for technical teams to hash out. Try to battle toe-to-toe against a number cruncher or bean counter, however, and you'll nearly always come up short.

Analytical?

You have a knack for breaking down concepts and aggregates into their component parts. To you, the city is a collection of streets and neighborhoods; and your annual salary consists of hourly pay rates plus perks for a car, travel, and other amenities.

Break every proposal from across the table into its constituent parts. Then make your recommendations about how to adjust some of those parts to be fairer to your side.

Assessment

Assess your own personality, including the strengths that seem most likely to work best for you in negotiations. Then test these strengths by practicing them on your friends. If they work, great! If you can't get your peers to agree to what you want, reassess your negotiating style and see if there isn't another part of your personality that can work better for you in negotiations.

TimeSaver

Sometimes the answer is right under your nose—and you don't even see it. Ask trusted friends and colleagues how they view your negotiating style. You may be surprised at their answers, but take not of the "whys" and "hows" of each response and use it to evaluate your performance at the next negotiations.

Aggressive?

If you've been successful so far by finding what you want and going for it any way you can, that style may serve you well in negotiations. You may be able to find tools and weapons you can use to win agreement to your main points. But also be aware that there can easily come a day when you stare across the table at an even more aggressive opponent with more experience, stronger tools and weapons, or even better luck on the day you meet.

Idealistic?

Many people succeed at negotiations by creating a vision of a cooperative venture where both sides contribute their best efforts and resources. Together, they achieve much success. Sometimes, this vision even comes true. But idealistic negotiators often can't communicate successfully with detail-minded or analytical types who can't see the forest because they're focused on all the trees.

Inclusive?

This breed of negotiator makes points with the other side by incorporating almost any idea, requirement, or strength into an ever-changing plan for getting great things accomplished. Yet this thinking style often means little to people who refuse to flex for every divergent element they encounter, and who instead want to focus on reaching a single, unchanging goal.

RELATED TOPICS

➤ Make Your Arguments Most Persuasive, (pages 28–29)

Inside Info

The power of silence works wonders in some negotiations. When the other side looks at you as though it's time for you to make an offer, just sit and smile expectantly. Think about your children, where you're going for dinner, or a recent ballgame, but don't say a word. Often times the other side will fill that silence with an offer that you can then use as a starting place for useful bargaining.

After You, I Insist . . .

In tic-tac-toe, whoever moves first has an easier time winning the game. In negotiations, it's often the opposite: The first person to make an offer is really making a big concession, and puts his or her side in a difficult position.

Here's why:

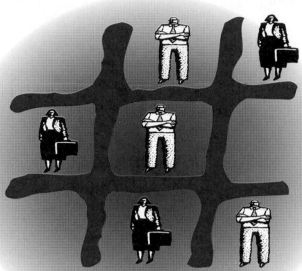

The Other Side Has More Information

Once you put an offer or draft agreement on the table, those on the other side have twice the information that you do. They already know their own bottom-line minimum, and now they know what you're suggesting. What's more, if they've done their homework, your initial offer gives them a pretty good guess at your own bottom-line minimum, too.

Strategic Advantage

If they respond with a counteroffer, they can place it strategically anywhere between what they hope to obtain and what you've already offered. Because it's keyed to what you first offered, their counteroffer reveals relatively little about the minimum arrangement they would accept.

Puts You on the Defensive

Or they may not bother to respond with a counteroffer. They can keep all their information close to their vest and simply work with your original offer. One ploy is to say something like: "That seems too high (or low) to us. How can you justify your offer?" Or they can try a tactic along the lines of: "That seems out of the ballpark to us. Can't you be a little more reasonable?" Either way, the negotiations stay focused on you and your expectations without the other side revealing anything equivalent to you.

WORDS TO LIVE BY

"Never mistake motion for action."

—Ernest Hemingway

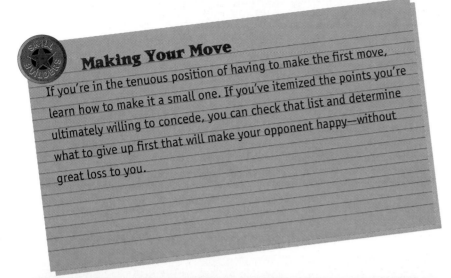

Making Your Move

If you're in the tenuous position of having to make the first move, learn how to make it a small one. If you've itemized the points you're ultimately willing to concede, you can check that list and determine what to give up first that will make your opponent happy—without great loss to you.

RED ALERT! Don't be forced into a position of having to give up too much up front. If your opponent balks at interaction, step back from the process by either reviewing a previous point or taking a break in the negotiations.

> **To prevent this, it's worth a lot of effort to put the other side in a position where they make the first offer.**

The simplest way to do this is to **ask for it** right off the bat. For example, you might make it a habit to say, as soon as a new round of negotiations get under way, "I think we're both pretty experienced and knowledgeable in this area, and we both know a fair agreement when we see one. Why don't you make us an offer we can accept without any serious haggling?"

If the other side does make an offer, you're immediately in a stronger position to get what you want.

If they're too smart to fall for this invitation, you can simply steer the negotiation away from making any offers of your own. **Delay and delay** until the other side finally puts an offer on the table.

Finally, you can just **play hardball.** If push comes to shove you can outwait the other side, refusing to make an offer when it's reasonably your turn to do so, for any number of reasons, such as:

"We don't have all the details we need yet to calculate exactly what our position ought to be. Why don't you suggest something?"

"We're reluctant to name a number because there are so many intangibles here. For instance, what would we do if . . ."

"We don't feel it's our place to make you an offer. We're here strictly to see what arrangements you're offering us."

RELATED TOPICS

➤ Small Concessions Can Make You a Winner, (pages 52–53)

Think twice before you commit. The give-and-take mentality of mutual concessions can easily put negotiators in the mindset of mutual harmony. Make sure you legitimately agree with each and every tenet of the negotiations before signing your final agreement.

Small Concessions Can Make You a Winner

Negotiation is essentially a process of giving things away to the other side. After all, if the other side doesn't want anything from you, or if it wants something you don't mind giving away, there's no need for any negotiation.

That's why the way in which you make concessions to the other side, the exact concessions you make, and what you receive in return are central elements in bringing any negotiation to a successful conclusion.

We pointed out earlier the importance of knowing what you want to achieve through negotiations and the fall-back levels from each of those ideal achievements. That's the list of concessions you're willing to make.

WORDS TO LIVE BY

"What seems to be generosity is often no more than disguised ambition, which overlooks a small interest in order to secure a great one."

—François Duc De La Rochefoucauld

Top Five Things to Concede

5. Use of client's name in all advertising.

4. Allow 90 day turnaround for payment.

3. 5% discount on orders over 1,000 units.

2. Pay transport costs on bulk orders.

1. Assign manager for this account only.

How and When to Offer Concessions

1 Offer your concessions in reverse priority order—the least important ones first.

When the other side offers to back away from a demand or give in to something you insist on, they'll probably ask for a concession from you in return. Be ready with an offer from your reverse priority list.

Make your offer of a concession before they can ask for something specific, because they're likely to ask for something more important than you're willing to give right now.

> "That's all well and good, but first we really need to concentrate on . . ."

2 Make every concession contingent on getting something in return from the other side.

Never say simply: "We'll reduce our requirements . . ." or "We won't insist on you doing . . . " Instead, frame every concession in terms of "If you agree to A, we'll give in on B."

The only exception is when the other side makes a contingent type of an exchange offer to you. But even then, you may want to counter with, "We'll accept A and B, but only if you also agree to C."

> "If you'll agree to the second quantity numbers, we'll consider the idea of a long-term contract."

3 Behave as though every concession is a loss of something vitally important to your side in the negotiations.

The other side puts its own values on the concessions it wants from you. But it should have no way of knowing precisely how important you feel each concession to be.

Thus, if you easily agree to a particular concession, they'll assume it's not important to you and may well push for more concessions in return for what they say is a big reduction in demands from their side of the table.

So treat every concession like it's your firstborn child. Give it up only with great reluctance, and make sure you demand something important in return from those across the table.

> "I'm sorry, but adding four more terminals will just add to our overhead, even if they're only $900.00 a piece."

Be wary of a negotiator who gives in too easily. He or she may simply be inexperienced or naive. But you may be making a deal with a person or organization that knows something you don't, or that plan may not to live up to the agreement.

Make doubly sure that you understand the implications of what you're agreeing to, and insist on including specific performance guarantees or penalties for any non-performance within the agreement.

RELATED TOPICS

➤ Trade One Concession for Another, (pages 20–21)

Keep in mind that your opponent may very well be examining the negotiations just as you are—using the "worst-case" method. It's important to realize that this form of preparation should not be perceived as undermining good faith in negotiations.

"Worst-Case" Scenarios

Most tough negotiations result in fairly complex agreements. While there's normally a basic quid pro quo—such as you deliver something and other side pays you for it—there may also be a great many contingency clauses, conditions, specifications, deadlines, and other factors that can come into play in various combinations.

By creating a "worst-case" scenario for the central agreement, you can uncover all the subagreements, multiple requirements, and minor specifications conditioned on other factors. This gives you the structure to analyze each section of the agreement using this worst-case magnifying glass.

Of course, the worst-case scenario probably won't happen. But examining it provides a quick and easy way to cast a new light on an agreement and spot any potential problems, flaws, weaknesses, or gaps in the terms you're presently considering. Here's how to do it:

1 Get clear in your mind what the specific part of the agreement you're considering binds each party to do. Perhaps you'll deliver something and the other party will pay you for it. Or you'll each perform some service for the other.

2 Now try to imagine the worst situation for you that the other side could possibly create.

- Fail to pay?
- Fail to perform?
- Steal your equipment?
- Share your secrets with a third party?

3 With this scenario in mind, evaluate how well the agreement performs for you.

- What are your options?
- Does it penalize the offending party?
- Does it give you recourse?
- Does it compensate you for lost time?

"Worst-Case" Scenario Matrix

Use a matrix like this one to check each agreement you negotiate. Each checked-off item means better protection in the event of a worst-case scenario.

	No Payment	Confidentiality Breach	Equipment Theft	Bad Performance
OPTIONS	✓	✓		
RECOURSE	✓			
PENALTY	✓			

Self-Monitoring

Naturally, you can walk through a worst-case mini scenario for any particular demand, concession, or arrangement the other side offers during the negotiations. Go through the same sort of evaluation from the other side's point of view. If you fail to perform as expected or put them in the worst possible situation, what sanctions do you face?

RELATED TOPICS

➤ Bad Temper, (pages 80–81)

➤ Take It or Leave It, (pages 84–85)

Inside Info

Keep the seating arrangement—and even meeting attendance—flexible within your team. For each session, let your expert on the matter under discussion sit closest to the team's lead negotiator. People whose special skills or knowledge won't be needed can sit farther away or can even skip the session entirely and save their energies for when they're most needed.

Control the Conference Setting

Previously we discussed how you can get a negotiation session to take place in your own facility, or at least one close by. By persuading your opponent to come onto your turf, you can take advantage of an extended set-up time, familiarity with the location, and the on-site support of management and staff. Once you have the meeting sited where you want it, make the best possible use of the location by considering the following four categories: seating, lighting, meals, and scheduling.

Seating

Set up the bargaining table so you and your team occupy the position of power or dominance. At most long tables, it's at one end. At unusually shaped tables, it's the position that's central and close to all of the other seats. At a round table, the position of power is determined by the surrounding walls, windows, audiovisual screens, and so forth.

Generally, it's best to have your team seated evenly on both flanks of the team leader. When teams get very large, it's often better to take fewer seats at the table, and set up rows of additional seating behind the main party.

Lighting

For daytime meetings, take care to diffuse the sun so it doesn't shine in anyone's eyes. Make sure to have adequate lighting in your meeting place so everyone can read documents easily and can clearly see the faces of all the individuals at the table. If you are working into the evening, keep the lights bright enough to maintain a high energy level, but don't go overboard with the florescents and turn the conference room into an interrogation room.

Meals

If you're serving food, establish menus that reinforce your bargaining stance. Excellent food, beautifully prepared, says you're successful and are taking these negotiations very seriously. Sandwiches, deli salads, or other quick-fix items declare the short amount of planning that goes into your decisions.

Take care not to serve heavy or rich foods that will make you tired and lethargic. Instead, try lighter foods like cold pasta dishes, fresh fruits, and vegetables. Resist the temptation to break up the sessions with an alcoholic beverage, as it not only alters judgment but is also dehydrating. Likewise, take it easy on the coffee and caffeinated beverages. That quick pick-me-up can also lay you flat in no time.

You can demonstrate your interest in doing business with your opponent by utilizing one of their services, products, or philosophies during a meal, if this is applicable. For example, if you are negotiating with an organization that has a strong environmental mentality, use real plates and flatware in place of paper plates, napkins, and plastic utensils.

TimeSaver
The use of place cards at the table is more than a polite formality. It ensures that all individuals sit where you strategically want them to be, and it prevents that nervous dance ritual which often occurs when people enter a conference room en masse.

Scheduling

You might feel the urge to play games with the schedule for negotiating sessions, taking advantage of the other side's jet lag or lack of sleep. Try to overcome this urge. Be solicitous of the other side's preferences and needs, and generally your opponent will reward you by entering the sessions with a win-win attitude.

RED ALERT! Often, your opponent may agree to come to your town but will insist on negotiations at a neutral location such as a hotel or business center.

Don't let this throw you. Visit the location far in advance to ensure that all your needs for the meetings will be met.

RELATED TOPICS

➤ **Use Your Home Court Advantage,** (pages 44–45)

Stay Focused on Your Goals

Inside Info

If the opposing party constantly focuses on points you consider minor rather than the major issues, it's possible you've misevaluated their situation, and what you think is a minor point is major to them.

You can test the other side's assessment of the importance of an issue by saying: "OK, we understand your point of view. If we substantially agree to what you're asking for, what concession will you make in return?"

If they offer little concession, you haven't learned very much; but if they offer a big one, you know that you have discovered an issue that's very important to the other side.

O ne of the ways experienced negotiators try to get more from the other side is by trying to confuse the main issue with minor points, unrelated matters, and distinctions that don't really make a difference.

That's why it's important to assemble an agenda and use it to keep discussions on a central path. A strategically prepared and thoroughly thought out agenda will help your side articulate its needs and will enable you to push talks steadily along toward a workable agreement.

WORDS TO LIVE BY

"Ignorant men don't know what good they hold in their hands until they've flung it away."

—Sophocles

Using an Agenda

Keep your major goals for the negotiation continually in place in front of you.

Refer to these goals whenever a new topic comes up.

If the new topic is more directly related to a major goal you're trying to achieve, it's OK to pursue it.

If the topic is less directly related to an important goal, it's probably a distraction you should avoid.

TimeSaver
Keep a rough accounting of the time you spend negotiating on each of the major issues. Whenever you and your negotiating opponent can't move forward on the present topic, switch to the major issue that has received the least attention so far. This tactic prevents time wasted on dead-end issues and allows both parties to revisit important issues at a later point in the proceedings.

Making It Clear

Practice responding to your negotiating opponent's attempts to muddy the waters by using phrases like:

"That's all well and good, but first we really need to concentrate on . . ."

"I can agree to whatever terms you propose on that matter, provided you say 'yes' right now to my suggestion regarding . . ."

"That issue will probably take care of itself once we agree about . . ."

RED ALERT!

Many opponents will question your agenda from the onset as a tactic, hoping to undermine your objectives and bully you into following their agenda. Don't fall for this. Instead, hear them out on their negotiating point and then refer back to the current item on your agenda.

RELATED TOPICS

➤ **Know What You Want to Achieve,** (pages 6–7)
➤ **Communicate Clearly,** (pages 22–23)

Inside Info

Keep a close watch on your opponents to pick up clues about what they want, what's important to them, and what they're trying to accomplish. Then, when a disagreement on some important point arises, you can "sweeten" the deal by suddenly offering a concession or an item that's not significant to you but is important enough to them to make a difference.

Creative Problem Solving

Most of the time, bargaining is simply a matter of trading one thing for another, one promise for another, or one compromise for another. Yet there are many situations in which there doesn't seem to be any middle ground on which to compromise. That's where creativity can save the day.

For example, suppose you're negotiating with the city for a permit to build a new home. The city limits the square footage of any home in that area, but you want considerably more space. There appears to be no room in the middle for a compromise. But a creative solution that satisfies both parties might be to design a home with an adjacent guest house. The city adheres to its ordinances, and you get your extra square footage.

Many times, creativity involves finding an new path through a maze of uncompromising positions. To gain success in negotiations by means of innovation and problem solving, remember to:

- **Look carefully for the underlying interests and demands of both sides.**
- **Look for a way to combine both sets of interests and demands into one proposal.**

WORDS TO LIVE BY

"All the works of man have their origin in creative fantasy. What right have we then to depreciate imagination?"

—Carl Jung

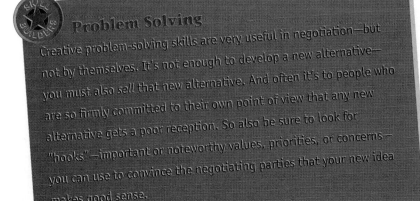

Problem Solving

Creative problem-solving skills are very useful in negotiation—but not by themselves. It's not enough to develop a new alternative—you must also *sell* that new alternative. And often it's to people who are so firmly committed to their own point of view that any new alternative gets a poor reception. So also be sure to look for "hooks"—important or noteworthy values, priorities, or concerns—you can use to convince the negotiating parties that your new idea makes good sense.

Top Ten Creative Locks

1 I don't have the right answer.
There isn't one, creative solution to any problem. Seeking that single-minded answer will stop you from brainstorming for other creative ends.

2 It's not logical.
Logic is valuable in analytical thinking but is restrictive in the creative phase of thinking.

3 But that's breaking the rules!
Most revolutionary thinkers have been the parents of rule-breaking ideas that break the traditional order of things.

4 That's not practical.
Practicality is the number-one killer of ideas.

5 Can't you see it my way?
Don't look at a solution in only one way. It's the quickest way to miss out on a smart alternative.

6 I don't want to do it wrong.
You can't do it right if you don't take risks. When you fail, you learn what doesn't work, which helps you to do a better job next time.

7 But this is work!
Yes, play has a role in the workplace. Playful attitudes generate a ton of creative ideas.

8 That's not my field.
True creative thinkers aren't restricted to their own area of expertise for a solution.

9 That's a foolish idea!
Many of the greatest thinkers of all time were scoffed at for having "foolish" ideas that were later recognized as "brilliant."

10 I'm not a creative person.
This type of negative thinking undermines any level of creativity a person may have. *Everyone* is creative in his or her own way.

RED ALERT! Negotiations are sometimes destined to fail because your opponent may have been unwillingly forced into the process. If this is the case, your most innovative and exciting creations often won't earn a second look.

Other people are very eager to make a deal but are legitimately stymied by lack of imagination, skill, physical factors, or other limitations on their ability to find a suitable compromise. In this case, your creative alternatives may be eagerly embraced if they meet the basic criteria of being reasonable, workable, and fair.

RELATED TOPICS

➤ **Get What You Really Want,** (pages 38–39)

➤ **Turning Around a Losing Trend,** (pages 96–97)

Inside Info

In negotiations, as in
almost everything else,
reward is usually com-
mensurate with risk. In
other words, if you're
playing things safe,
going for "sure deals"
every time, and doing
nothing to jeopardize
negotiating success,
you're probably leaving
more on the table than
most other negotiators
would have done.

Getting Comfortable with Acceptable Risk

Because good negotiation is about compromise and concession, many people never consider the vast amount of risk involved in certain negotiations. But there's often plenty. For example:

Lawyers are negotiating for a plea bargain for their client. The risk is that they will accept a greater penalty than a better negotiator could have arranged.

You're buying an expensive item, like a car or a house. The risk is that you will pay more than a better negotiator could have won.

You're trying to nail down an important business contract. The risks include paying too much, getting too little, agreeing to terms that involve hidden aggravations, or blowing the deal if you're too demanding.

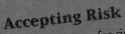

Accepting Risk

Increase your tolerance for risk in these three important ways:

1. Practice putting yourself in riskier situations where the penalty for losing will be small.
2. Practice relaxation exercises while facing risk in your negotiation sessions.
3. Create fallback positions for each risky position you take.

1 For example, bargain aggressively at a flea market for a $25 item. As you get comfortable with higher levels of risk, you can increase the stakes.

3 For example, if you ask the other side for three times what you think is a justifiable reduction in price, be prepared to ask again for only as much of a discount as you think you ought to get. By focusing on your fallback position, you'll make your face and language relatively calm, effectively masking from those across the table the real level of risk you think you're assuming.

2 Visualize a calm scene, relax each muscle group in your body, practice deep breathing, chant, and do everything else you can think of to lessen the sensation of risk. The more you relax while facing risk, the more risk you'll be able to endure with comfort.

Be ready to "step off" when the other side becomes too demanding, too difficult, or just plain uncompromising. Successful deals contain something beneficial for all parties. If you can't get the people across the negotiating table to consider what you want, why get involved in the first place?

RELATED TOPICS

➤ Keep Your Expectations Reasonable, (pages 36–37)

One good thing about conciliation is that you don't need an immediate payback from each one of them. Instead, you can sprinkle them through-out the negotiation process, each time build-ing up your general level of credit and credibility, otherwise known as good faith or good intent.

Offering small concessions in a conciliatory manner allows the other side to tally up small, meaningful points that they want—and you don't mind giving away. Then, when you want a larger point from them, they'll be more inclined to give it to you in a spirit of goodwill.

"I do not want people to be agreeable, as it saves me the trouble of liking them."

—Jane Austen

The Art of Conciliation

There's a fine but important difference between making a concession (a compromise) in return for some equivalent concession by the other side, and offering a conciliation (a giveaway of something you profess to be important). The main impact of this difference? Instead of asking for a direct compromise on negotiated terms in return, you're asking to change the subject under discussion, or to speed up the flow of the negotiations toward a useful conclusion.

The proper use of conciliation begins by keeping track of sore points across the table: compromises the other side has made, small concessions they want that you don't want to give, points they've agreed to that they now regret, and so forth. Day by day, these sore points add up until you have a formidable list of potential conciliations.

Now, when the negotiations reach an impasse or you want to move them forward at least one giant step, you're in a position to make a bold offer of conciliation. Naturally, you'll first offer only the most harmless of these points.

For example, you might say something like, "Last week, Ms. Fuentes, you were pressing me for our production costs. If you're willing to let this subject go, I can agree to move your project up several weeks on the schedule." Or you could press more directly for a final "yes or no" vote on the entire negotiated agreement toward which you're working.

The power of a sudden conciliation on a point the opposition has given up as lost can lead to a major change in the flow of negotiations—particularly when they are otherwise stalled.

List of Concessions

1. Production line controls will be eased
2. Specific health care privileges
   - family plans more comprehensive
   - dental plans
   - therapeutic/mental health plans
3. Increase O.T. Pay
4. Renegotiate November's pay agreements

Timing

Practice making a conciliation in a sudden, lightning strike. Make your introductory remarks about where you'd like the negotiations to go next, but leave the point on which you're ready to give in until the end. Finish with something like "We'll concede on . . ." or "We'll agree to all you asked for on . . ." Then sit back and gauge the effect of this thunderbolt.

Conciliation can backfire as rapidly as it can operate in your favor. If the other side begins to stockpile small concessions you toss their way, the concessions may be adding up to be one greater point that you may not have been so eager to part with.

CASE IN POINT

Logical Manufacuring is negotiating with Tasteful Timepieces to form a new partnership. Logical manufactures kitchen appliances and wants Tasteful to install the clock/food timers for the bulk, reduced rate. Tasteful wants a bonus package based on the overall sales of the appliances, while Logical only wants to pay a flat fee, plus a bonus if 50,000 units are sold.

Logical wants to do business with Tasteful, so it begins to offer small pieces of the bonus package. First, it agrees to use the Tasteful logo in all the print advertising for the product. Tasteful is appreciative, but its negotiator doesn't feel that they can give Logical a discounted rate. Then Logical promises to give tasteful the first bid on their new series of appliances. Tasteful agrees to give Logical a partially reduced rate, and they come to an agreement.

In reality, Logical only gave Tasteful a fraction of what they originally asked for. But the conciliatory gestures underscored the good faith in which Logical was entering into the agreement, and Tasteful was appeased.

➤ Trade One Concession for Another, (pages 20–21)

The Art of Debate

Negotiation and debate are inextricably intertwined. But they are not the same thing. As you've seen elsewhere in this book, there are many aspects of negotiation that have nothing to do with debate, which is a formal argument over opposing points of view. Yet argument is frequently a central feature of negotiations and can be a powerful force for getting the other side to agree to what you want.

To help you master the art of debate and use it more effectively during negotiations, four essential elements and techniques are listed to the right.

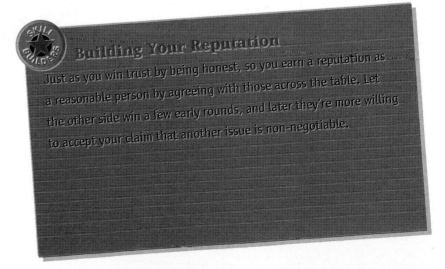

Building Your Reputation

Just as you win trust by being honest, so you earn a reputation as a reasonable person by agreeing with those across the table. Let the other side win a few early rounds, and later they're more willing to accept your claim that another issue is non-negotiable.

Debate
Elements and Techniques

Prioritize

This refers to the shape and form of the topic under debate, and the relative placement and importance of the supporting arguments. To develop structure, you must learn to:

- Listen to what the other side is saying
- Find strengths and weaknesses in their arguments and factual material
- Determine what issues and arguments are most important
- Prioritize what's important
- Plan the best ways to defend your central issues and win the arguments you need

Straw Man

A classic debating technique is to set up an unimportant argument, and then prove it false. Watch for others using this technique against you. For example, if you're negotiating for higher wages, the employer's stringent dress code could be a perfect straw man. Whichever side argues about it, either for or against, is wasting its energy and diverting its attention from more important issues. At the proper moment, the other side boldly points out: "No, no. You're wasting your time. That's not the important issue. What's really important is . . ."

Change the Subject

It's a time-honored debating strategy to bring up a new issue when you're losing on the present one. Instead of trying to answer an unanswerable question, you find a way to talk about another issue entirely. Sometimes you can apply that unanswerable question to the new topic. Sometimes you have to work along the lines of "That reminds me of this other thing . . ."

Socratic Method

Thousands of years ago, Socrates got his students to understand complex issues and come to the proper conclusions by asking them a series of questions, the answers to which inevitably led those listening exactly where he wanted them to go.

The technique still works if you have the intellect, the preparation, and the willpower to force your series of questions into the debate when and where needed.

RED ALERT! Beware of the other side misinterpreting your position. You say you want a ten-day vacation, but your boss is opposed. In the heat of argument, he insists he can't give anyone two weeks off during the busy season. It takes a sharp ear to hear him misinterpret ten days as two weeks, but it's important to keep the other side arguing on issues of real substance, not fake ones they may intentionally or unintentionally invent.

RELATED TOPICS

➤ **Make Your Arguments Most Persuasive,** (pages 28–29)

The Art of Persuasion

When all is said and done, a person with a great deal of persuasive ability will strike a better deal than a person without it. Some persuasion is based on native charm, of course, just like some sports success is based on native ability. But the most successful negotiators are those who have cultivated their natural abilities and learned how to make the most of them. That's why studying and practicing the art of persuasion are great ways to improve your success as a negotiator.

Practice using the elements of persuasion in your negotiating proposals, your responses to the other side's proposals, and your back-and-forth discussion of important issues. Persuasion in a negotiation works like seasonings in a recipe: They make a dish more attractive to the senses and more enjoyable when eaten. As long as you don't use too much, you can use them at every meal.

The main elements of persuasion include trust, reward, and logic.

Trust

First, demonstrate your trustworthiness by scrupulously avoiding lies, manipulations, half-truths, and the like.

Second, demonstrate your trust in the other side by taking their word on a particular point, and by keeping any suspicions you may have to yourself.

The best way to build trust is *through* time, by demonstrating your integrity and honesty in relationships with the people sitting across the table.

A reputation for being trustworthy will often precede you into important negotiations, increasing the level of trust fairly quickly, even among total strangers.

Reward

The art of "sweetening" a deal is a beautiful thing. Most people are ready to accept other peoples' terms in a negotiation—if you can make it "worth their while." That's why good negotiators study their opponents, try to find out what makes them tick, and constantly search for things they can say, do, or give to the other side that will, in turn, reward them.

RED ALERT!

Although it is less elegant than other methods of persuasion, a threat—particularly the threat of losing something important—is a great motivator.

But threats should be used judiciously, and only as a last resort. Don't consider using a threat if you're not prepared to follow through with it. If your opponent calls your bluff, you could not only destroy current negotiations but also sabotage any future dealings with your opponent.

Logic

The logic of history	The logic of self-interest	The logic of debate	The logic of analysis

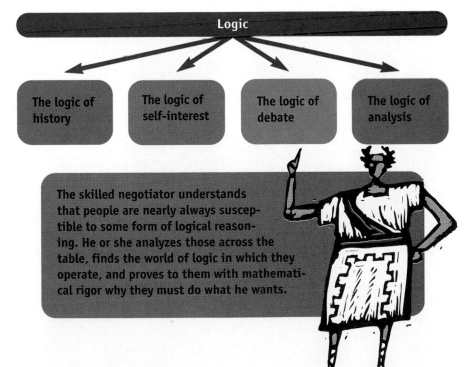

The skilled negotiator understands that people are nearly always susceptible to some form of logical reasoning. He or she analyzes those across the table, finds the world of logic in which they operate, and proves to them with mathematical rigor why they must do what he wants.

RELATED TOPICS

➤ **Make Sure the Other Side Hears You,** (pages 30–31)

Body Language

Earlier, we discussed how important it is to keep everyone on your side of the table not only in sync but also alert to the subtle messages they may be sending to your negotiating opponents.

Many of those messages can be transmitted through body language, a subtle but important form of communication. As you likely know from your own experience, a person's facial expression, tone of voice, limbs, and body posture can—and usually do—convey a world of detail about what he or she is thinking, feeling, and planning. This is the sort of detail that gives one side in a negotiation a major advantage over the other.

To become a more skillful and successful negotiator, study your own body language and practice reading the body language of others. The following four elements should all be considered:

1 Posture

The more erect postures, with upper bodies leaning forward, generally indicate readiness for action, perhaps even fear or anger. It's the well-known "flight or fight" syndrome with which we are born. In contrast, bodies leaning back, slumped, or even laying down show a willingness to communicate, or at least not to leave immediately. Putting together information you get from face, voice, limbs, and posture, you can often learn quite a bit about your negotiating opponent that he or she wouldn't voluntarily reveal.

Mirroring

"Mirroring" works by getting people to feel comfortable with you. Basically, mirroring is putting your own body in the same position and posture as the person you are talking to. When calling attention to yourself, move slowly and try to 1) adjust your breathing rate, 2) position your body, and 3) move your arms and legs in a manner compatible to the other party. You'll notice how the other person will eventually relax and become more agreeable.

2 Facial expression

The face, and particularly the eyes, are like a window on what you're thinking and feeling. The more absorbed you are in your own thoughts and emotions, the clearer that window becomes.

Watch other people as they make their points. This may "tell you" what they're interested in, what they want. The more animated their face and eyes, the closer their words match their thoughts and feelings.

RED ALERT!

The degree to which individuals have an understanding and mastery of their body language varies greatly. Estimate the other person's ability to disguise his or her true body language, and give what you read in movements and voice only as much credence as you feel it deserves.

3 Tone of voice

Voice is an audio analog to the face. It conveys emotion, honesty, and vulnerability in great depth. But voices can deceive—often more easily than faces—so use this clue only as one among many.

4 Limb position

Classically speaking, crossed arms and legs indicate withdrawal and defensiveness—a difficult attitude for successful negotiations. Open arms and legs show a more receptive attitude—a willingness to listen and perhaps even reach agreement.

Arms and hands are separately expressive and can reveal inner thoughts and feelings through a wide range of motions—from gentle and subdued to energetic and enthusiastic to angry and aggressive.

RELATED TOPICS

➤ What's Your Negotiating Style?, (pages 48–49)

Know When It's Time to Quit

One of the cardinal rules of the salesperson is to recognize when you've completed the sale and immediately leave before you say something that will undo what you've already accomplished.

The same rule—with a little more complexity—applies in negotiations. There are at least five different reasons why you should terminate negotiations, and every one of them works to your advantage. Remember, "quitting" negotiations is not always your last move. It's just a powerful one.

1 *When the other party is unreasonable*
Many negotiators, particularly those who feel they are in a position of power, expect you to meet unreasonable demands and requirements.

For a while, you'll want to talk with these people in good faith. But when you realize they're not interested in compromise or concession, you may decide that further negotiations are a complete waste of your time. As soon as you recognize this, it's time to leave.

2 *To get away from a bully*
Some people have an aggressive negotiating style of badgering, yelling, and bullying the opposition in hopes of getting a better deal.

You may be willing to tolerate some of this behavior, but you may reach your limit. That's when you say: "I'm tired of the way you're treating me. The next time you try to bully or browbeat me, I'm leaving." Often this will end the obnoxious behavior. But if it doesn't, pack up and leave at once.

3 *When you make a last offer*
There's nothing more cheesy than having someone make you a last offer and, when it's rejected, stick around to make yet another one.

Be cautious about making any threats in negotiations, particularly ones about "this is my last offer." But if you feel the situation is ripe and you're not making progress any other way, go ahead and make a last offer. If it's not accepted, be sure to leave.

RED ALERT!

Be leery of the blustery opponent who gets visibly frustrated and threatens to pull out of the process altogether. More times than not, this person is trying to manipulate you into conceding on issues to keep the negotiations alive. By keeping a clear vision of what you ultimately want, you can remain insulated from this disturbing and interruptive ploy.

4 *As a negotiating ploy*
There are some negotiators who use this trick in nearly every round of talks. But like in the fable, Peter and the Wolf, you can quit only so many times before you build a much-deserved reputation for grandstanding.

Save this tactic for when negotiations reach an impasse and you just can't come to an agreement. Then, quitting may be the right approach for both parties—enabling them to sit back and rethink their objectives.

5 *When you've gotten a good deal*
This is perhaps the most common mistake that inexperienced negotiators make. They continue to negotiate after they've gotten everything they originally wanted. Don't do this.

Think of your negotiations as a mountain climb. When you reach the summit, there's nowhere to go but down. Instead, hitch a helicopter ride back home and celebrate what you've accomplished.

RELATED TOPICS

➤ Take It or Leave It, (pages 84–85)

➤ It's OK to Walk, (pages 86–87)

Inside Info

Partners tend to be more alike and agreeable with each other than a good guy/bad guy situation indicates. If you see such extremes of temperament acted out for you by people who work closely together, you're probably the subject of some highly motivated role-playing. It's not real.

Good Guy/Bad Guy Role-Playing

You know the famous good cop/bad cop scene that appears in almost every police show on TV? One partner pretends to be mean, angry, vicious, and impossible to deal with. After thoroughly confusing or frightening the subject, the other partner comes in and pretends to be the exact opposite. "I don't know how long I can hold my partner back," the good cop says. "Can't you please give me something useful, so I can use it when I try to reason with him?"

This scenario sounds a lot dumber than it plays out in real life. That's because the bad cop does everything he can to unsettle the people on the other side of the negotiating table. Rattled, they don't always perceive the game being run against them.

Now that you're forewarned, of course, you'll never fall for it. But just in case someone pulls it on you, here are some pointers:

WORDS TO LIVE BY

"Never give a sucker an even break."
—W. C. Fields

Practice Role-Playing

If you want to try the good guy/bad guy tactic, keep these points in mind:

- You must have a partner who can believably act out at least one role. By far the toughest role to assume is the "bad" guy.
- You and your partner should agree in advance on exactly what you're trying to extract from the other side.

Have a few signals between you, so that you can fine-tune the performance as it's happening. A few words or hand signals work for concepts like: "try again now," "push harder," "push softer," and "let me take over."

You don't have to deal with the bad guy at all. As long as there are two of them—which is the strong point of this game—you can simply refuse to talk to anyone but the nice guy. By making this stick, you pull the teeth of the good guy/bad guy approach.

You can go with the game and turn it against them. You can pretend to be so rattled, confused, and frightened by the bad guy that you can't think straight, you don't know what to do, and you want to break off all negotiations right away. Try this response and you'll be amazed at how quickly the "bad guy" attitude evaporates.

CASE IN POINT

You've decided to buy two new computers for your office and, after calling around, decide to go to the local computer supermart which promises to "meet or beat" any competitor's advertised price.

The salesperson helps you select the model. Because you're buying two, you ask for a volume discount. "We're already giving you our lowest price," he says. "We already beat ElectroMart's price by $50."

You consider what he's saying, realizing that you could beat his price by $100 by buying from mail order, but you want the computer's today. "I guess I'll just go home and think about it," you bluff. He quickly responds, "let me go talk to my supervisor about this."

When he returns, the salesperson says, "My supervisor says we've got an overstock on these, so I can give you another $50 off each computer if you buy the extended warranty for $200." Since your office already has a service contract, you don't need the extra warranty. "Thanks, but no thanks," you tell him, and prepare to walk.

"Let me talk to my supervisor again," he says. "I'm sure we can come up with something." He returns, with the supervisor in tow. She asks, "I'd like to let you walk home with these computers today. How can we close the deal?"

RELATED TOPICS

➤ Bluffing, (pages 78–79)

➤ Intimidation, (pages 82–83)

Stonewalling is a perfect tactic if you are under no pressure to reach an agreement because things are just fine as they are. For example, if you own a small gold mine and you're making $1 million a year, you don't have to sell it. You can simply stonewall until you get a purchase offer that seems attractive to you.

If this describes the people across the table from you, there's little you can do except sweeten your offer a little at a time to see if you can engage their interest. If your best offer isn't better than what they have, there's probably no rational way to negotiate an agreement.

Stonewalling

If you like banging your head into a stone wall, you'll love dealing with a person across the negotiating table who doesn't change his mind, doesn't reduce his demands, or provide any reasonable flexibility on any terms of the proposed agreement.

It's the exact opposite of what negotiations are supposed to be: even-handed, fair-minded give-and-take between reasonable people.

Many reasonable people use stonewalling as a tactic, secretly hoping to make a deal with you after they've softened you up with a super-tough demeanor.

People generally do this because it has brought them good deals in the past. But it works best against inexperienced negotiators, and against parties desperate to make a deal. If you maintain your cool, are not desperate, and have some alternatives, you can negotiate in a way whereby stonewalling won't hurt you.

Breaking Through Stonewalling

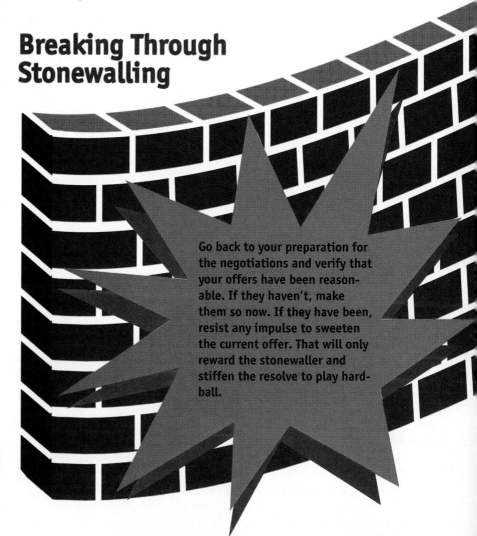

Go back to your preparation for the negotiations and verify that your offers have been reasonable. If they haven't, make them so now. If they have been, resist any impulse to sweeten the current offer. That will only reward the stonewaller and stiffen the resolve to play hardball.

Set a limit on the negotiations. For example, you might make six tries at reaching a compromise with the stonewaller on a particular point. Once you reach the limit, break off negotiations by saying something like: "I can see you're not willing to be reasonable. I'll just have to go elsewhere for a deal. If you ever want to negotiate more reasonably, call me."

Ask them to justify their unwillingness to be flexible. Press the other side to explain why they won't budge, why they won't compromise, why they won't accept adjustments in terms. If they offer no explaination, you're no worse off than before.

People favor stonewalling for many reasons. They may hope it will lower your expectations or force you into a mistaken concession that favors their side.

They may want to delay negotiations until a time more favorable for them. Or they may simply have no idea what's fair, and plan to accept whatever you offer just before you quit negotiating and leave in disgust.

That's why it's important to meet stonewalling tactics with increased toughness, and not with any conciliation.

RELATED TOPICS

➤ **Worst Case Scenarios,** (pages 54–55)

➤ **It's OK to Walk,** (pages 86–87)

Inside Info

Because bluffing can backfire, don't bluff on a negotiating point which could prove disasterous if you lost.

Bluffing

American lore, and particularly Western lore, is full of the art of bluffing. Card players bluffing others into folding, despite their higher cards; lawmen bluffing gunslingers into giving up, despite their greater skill at gunplay; unwilling heroes bluffing the enemy into making a mistake, despite their superior position at the time, and so on.

At bottom, a bluff is a false statement you make to the other side—not always a lie, but certainly an exaggeration. Unable to prove your statement is false, the other side eventually concedes something important to you.

But while the ability to bluff is often considered a sign of chutzpah, it's not a totally favorable way to pursue negotiations. It brings with it some

serious flaws:

The bluff.
A bluff by one side invites a bluff by the other. Bluffing your negotiating opponent is really a form of brinkmanship, where a single misstep can throw you over a cliff to smash on the rocks below.

The other side refuses to concede.
You may have no choice but to follow through on your bluff by changing your own demands, taking back a concession you've previously given away, or calling off the negotiations entirely if the other side does not concede. If you're not ready to do this, again your credibility is damaged. If you are ready to do this, it may put you in a position you'd rather not be in.

Getting caught.
If the other side is able to examine your bluff, you may soon be revealed as a liar, or at least an exaggerator, damaging your credibility. And remember, you may also feel embarrassed about being caught.

WORDS TO LIVE BY

"Observe your enemies lest they first find out your faults."
—Antisthenes

Successfully working a bluff into your negotiating strategy clearly takes a great deal of self-control, a tolerance for risk, and keen judgment about the other party's state of mind and desire for agreement. 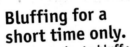 the other side successfully by:

How is a bluff different from a lie? It isn't, really. Ex- cept that a bluff is a highly specialized form of lying, usually made within the confines of a particular situation—a game of cards, for example, or a negotia- tion— and intended solely to force the other side into giving you an advantage within that situation. If you have serious compunctions about lying, don't bluff.

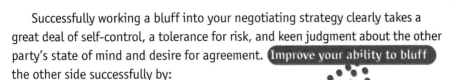

Bluffing intensely.
Bluffs work best when you put your heart and soul into them. If your facial expression or a trembling hand gives your bluff away, the other side gets an easy victory.

Bluffing for a short time only.
It's far easier to bluff your opponent in a way that lets you maintain that a lie is the truth only for a short time.

For example, you could say something like: "If you can't agree to these terms, these negotiations are over. I'll be back at my hotel. Call me there by eight o'clock tomorrow morning if your answer is 'yes.' Otherwise, I'm flying back home."

Bluffing selectively.
If you try to bluff your negotiating opponent all the time, the other side will soon catch on and ignore all future statements you can't back up with facts.

RELATED TOPICS

➤ The Power of Deadlines, (pages 34–35)

➤ Take It or Leave It, (pages 84–85)

Don't allow your oppo-
nent's bad temper to rub
off on you. There's no
reason to become defen-
sive or modify your nego-
tiating position just
because they're yelling
and banging the table. It
takes a certain amount
of experience, and will-
power, to hold to this idea
under the pressure of a
cranky opponent. But it's
basic—and integral—
to your success.

*"It is human
nature to hate
him whom you
have injured."*
—Tacitus

Bad Temper

So far, we've discussed negotiations in terms of a civilized, fair-minded discussion between rational and reasonable people. In the real world of negotiations, however, there are plenty of people who show an amazingly bad temper.

- Some of them are just plan grouchy, cranky, or negative.
- Others are having a bad day.
- A few use bad temper as a negotiating tactic to help them browbeat the other side into giving up more than they normally would.

As with other tactics designed to make you back down, the worst thing you can possibly do is try to make life easier for the ones with the bad tempers. That's just what they want, and you'll not only be rewarding them for uncivilized behavior, you'll be giving up negotiating points that you would otherwise want to retain.

> There are two strategies that are far more effective in dealing with bad-tempered negotiators across the table from you.

You can fight fire with fire, and show just as much bad temper as you are being shown.

If you've been treated badly for a while, you can probably reach down into your own true emotions and drag up some real anger that you can display for the other side. If not, you can try to put on a show as good as the one you're watching. Raise your voice, use extreme hand motions, perhaps even bang something to make a loud noise for emphasis.

If the other side has been faking, they may suddenly try to calm you down. But regardless of how they react, your show of anger will abruptly change the mood of the negotiations.

You can switch to the thera-pist/caretaker role, in which you show genuine concern for the other side's bad temper, but don't let it influence your behavior or sway you from your agenda.

With this strategy, you take an emotional step back from the negotiating table. Less engaged in what the other side is saying and doing, you can begin to observe them a little more analytically, and calculate what you want to say and do to achieve the goal you're after.

CASE IN POINT

Angry Al
Rants and flares nostrils. Believes whatever you're getting out of the deal entitles him to scream at you.

Snappy Sharon
Makes irritating put-downs at every possible chance. In kind, responses elicit ice-cold stares.

Dissatisfied Dave
This one is a quiet grump. Pours over facts and data pertinent to the deal looking for a chance to gripe.

Screaming Ed
This yeller wants you to know he's in charge of the negotiations. Warning: sit as far away as possible.

Abusive Kate
Has equally abusive boss. Needs to take her frustration out on someone, usually you!

Barking Bob
A psychotic Negotiator from Hell! Nothing short of total capitulation will make this guy happy. Run away!!!

Sullen Sue
Makes Unhappy Angela look like a saint. You'll never know what's eating at this negotiator.

Carping Carl
Will remind you time and again about how much his side has given up. Always needs one more concession.

Unhappy Angela
Manages to manipulate the negotiations with her frequent mood swings. Be ready for a wild ride.

RED ALERT!

People who use bad temper as a negotiating tactic tend to spring it on their opponents. People who are genuinely upset, angry, or tired of having a headache tend to show a slowly deteriorating mood that you can see developing during the negotiating session. They probably deserve a little more sympathy than the person who seems happy enough, and then suddenly erupts in a fit of anger. More than likely, you're watching a show.

RELATED TOPICS

➤ Timing is Everything, (pages 40–41)

➤ Know When It's Time to Quit, (pages 72–73)

Inside Info

The main source of your resistance to threats and intimidation in negotiations will be your feelings of security—not just personal security, which is important, of course, but feelings of security you gain from having a safe, strong negotiating position that will not be hurt too badly, even if the threats and intimidation are actually carried out by the other side.

Intimidation

Whether we like it or not, threats and intimidation are a normal part of human interaction. They may not be pleasant or fair, but they do exist, and to be a successful negotiator you must learn to avoid being sidetracked or harmed by them. Let's consider some different kinds of threats and intimidation, and discuss how best to respond to each one.

Playing Unfairly

Threats of bringing in the "big guns"

Often the other side will threaten to bring higher-level people into negotiations to bargain with your management. In most cases, the unspoken threat is that your boss will not be happy when he or she hears you couldn't conclude the negotiations without their help.

The best response is not to show any indication that you're bothered by this threat. Perhaps there's no reason to worry, since such a change won't compromise your position when the negotiations are over. But even if it will, conceding to unreasonable demands will not enhance your reputation as a negotiator, either. Instead, call their bluff and behave as though you're not concerned about this threat. Generally, this will either end or reduce the chances that the other side will carry out their threat.

Threats of canceling the negotiations

Depending on the circumstances, this may be a threat you don't want carried out. But if you have alternative sources for what you want, a break in the negotiations may not be so bad for your side. And if the other side has fewer options than you do, this may be just another empty threat.

WORDS TO LIVE BY

". . . the only thing we have to fear is fear itself."
—Franklin D. Roosevelt

Maintaining Personal Space

Due to cultural differences, you may find yourself intimidated by an opponent who doesn't share the same concept of personal space as you. If someone is standing too close, don't assume that this is a threat or aggressive gesture. Practice taking a step backward, or moving so that an object, such as a table, comes between you. If this doesn't work, try saying, "Excuse me, but you're standing a bit close for my comfort." If the person isn't trying to strong-arm you, he or she will respect your request and step back.

If you have skeletons in your closet that can be used against you, be careful about the type of person with whom you negotiate important matters. Certain people are in the habit of getting their own way through intimidation and threats. If you must deal with them, it's better not to be guarding any secrets they can hold over your head.

Playing Dirty

Threats of revealing your secrets

It's the principle behind blackmail, and it works. Assuming you're guarding some secret you don't want others to know, the threat of revealing it will have a powerful influence on your willingness to make concessions during tough negotiations. If this is the case, the best solution for your side is to have another person replace you at the negotiating table. This lets the air out of your opponent's balloon and forces him or her to look at the issues at hand, not just the game playing.

Threats of physical harm

If you're negotiating with someone who threatens to harm you physically, you should ask yourself, "Why am I negotiating with this person?" If you believe that you are in immediate danger, call on someone who can protect you: The police, corporate security, or even the presence of an impartial witness can diffuse the situation long enough for you to regain your composure.

If you must negotiate with this individual, increase the level of force on your side. Add people to your team, videotape the negotiations as an "instructional video" for lower-level team members, or have a security person make "routine" checks on the conference room. Just presenting the possibility of equal and opposite force is often enough to keep threats against you from becoming actions.

RELATED TOPICS

➤ Stay Focused on Your Goals, (pages 58–59)

➤ Turning Around a Losing Trend, (pages 96–97

"Take it or leave it" proposals can come at the beginning, middle, or end of a round of negotiations. At the beginning, they are most often a test to see how you respond and to gauge the strength of your side's bargaining position.

In the middle, they may well be a true expression of the other side's frustration, or their inability to give any more concessions and still come away happy with the deal.

At the end, they are often a last-minute tactic employed by the other side to rush you into a concession you don't want to make in order to salvage all you've put into the negotiations so far.

Take It or Leave It

This is a favorite tactic for people who feel they have a much stronger negotiating position than you, or who personally enjoy a bullying style of bargaining rather than a discussion between relative equals. Such a stance goes directly against the general concept of negotiations, which is fair-minded give-and-take toward a mutually satisfying agreement. But while a "take it or leave it" offer often signals the end of any chance for a fair agreement, it doesn't have to.

There are several ways to react to a "take it or leave it" proposal coming at you from across the negotiating table. You can:

Ignore it

Many times, a "take it or leave it" proposal is sent across the bargaining table as a trial balloon—to see how your side will react. Since you can't know if this is the motivation, your best response is first to ignore it. Just keep negotiating as though you didn't hear the "take it or leave it" demand. To those across the table, this will look as though you're a tough, seasoned negotiator who is convinced of the strength of his or her own position. If they never intended to insist on their "take it or leave it" demand, they'll follow along, pretending it never happened and entering into earnest negotiations with you.

Send back one just like it

Another response is to respond in kind. Rather than "take it" or "leave it," you create your own "take it or leave it" proposal and put it forward as forcefully as you know how. If the other side has been testing you, this response will seem to be proof that you're a tough-minded negotiator. If they honestly expected you to yield to their proposal, they'll now have to rethink their own position and decide on their next move.

TimeSaver
If you have the upper hand in negotiations, you can quickly assume the leadership position by employing a "take it or leave it" proposal.

A lthough this may seem to be an obvious point, don't present a "take it or leave it" proposal to the other side unless you are sincerely prepared for the other side to "leave" it.

Demand a good-faith concession

One of the most powerful responses to a "take it or leave it" proposal is to appear angry and offended, insist that the proposal is proof the other side is not negotiating in good faith, and demand they make an immediate concession on some point of contention as proof that they sincerely want to reach a fair agreement.

This is likely to be such an unexpected response that you will catch the other side unprepared; and it may turn the tables in your favor.

Submit

If you've tried not to give in to your negotiating opponent's "take it or leave it" offer and you now believe their proposal is for real, then face it: You have only those two fairly obvious choices. Consider selecting whichever one of them is in your best interest. But give preference to the "leave it" option, since you can almost always come back again and accept what you previously had declined.

RELATED TOPICS

➤ Assess Your Opponent's Strengths and Weaknesses, (pages 18–19)

➤ Keep Your Expectations Reasonable, (pages 36–47)

It is definitely OK to walk during a negotiation. But it doesn't work quite so well if you walk out too often.

That's why it's important you pick your spot. The best points on which to walk out on include:

- The last point you want before you agree to the entire deal.

- The most important point you want in the agreement, without which you'd rather not sign.

- A crucial part of the negotiating process, such as submitting disagreements to arbitration.

It's OK to Walk

This may be one of the most important points you can learn about negotiations, and one of the strongest tactics you can use. All you need to do is behave as though you've reached the limit of what you can agree to. It doesn't matter whether you're talking about price, terms, delivery dates, or other issues. You state your proposal and then bargain for a while, earnestly trying to get the other side to meet you on an agreement. After two or three refused offers, you can say something like, "I'm sorry we couldn't make a deal here. But thanks anyway." And you walk out the door!

You'll be surprised how often the other side will stop you before you can get all the way through that door. Whatever excuse they use to call you back, you both know they've tacitly admitted they want the deal more than you. After that, it's mainly a matter of you keeping up the pressure toward the proposal you've made. Quite often, they'll finally agree to it. Once you begin walking, three things might happen:

The other party can stop you before you complete your walk. In this case, you've won a major victory and established yourself in a powerful position to get exactly what you want.

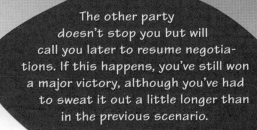

The other party doesn't stop you but will call you later to resume negotiations. If this happens, you've still won a major victory, although you've had to sweat it out a little longer than in the previous scenario.

Backpedaling

If the other side lets you walk, you may wind up making the call to continue negotiations. If so, find a good explanation for why things have changed. The worst possible reason is to say: "I thought things over and I guess you were right." Instead, practice saying something like, "My needs have changed, and I'm only looking for half of the quantity," or "My situation has changed, and those issues aren't so important anymore."

"My needs have changed, and I'm only looking for half of the quantity."

"My situation has changed, and those issues aren't so important anymore."

The other party doesn't stop you and doesn't call later. In this case, the ball is squarely in your court. You can let the negotiations end, perhaps looking elsewhere for what you want, or you can make the call. If you handle it right, you won't lose too much ground and you can still bargain hard for some of the points you want.

RELATED TOPICS

> The Art of Conciliation, (pages 64–65)

Many people try to negotiate from the very beginning by "low balling"—offering an unfairly low proposal—or its opposite, "high balling." They expect either to get what they want from an negotiating opponent who can't fight them to a fair agreement, or by "splitting the difference" later on. There are two things you can try to defeat this approach. You can:

- Call attention to the unfairly high or low nature of the other side's proposals from the very beginning.

- Note how many concessions the other side had made from their original offer, and point out that it's fewer and less meaningful concessions than you have made. This will lay the groundwork for you to refuse to accept a "split the difference" proposal toward the end of the negotiations.

Splitting the Difference

This is a common negotiating tactic that often seems fair to the uninitiated but may paint you into a corner if you're not careful. The basic idea is to take the difference between the last two offers and divide this in half to find a "middle ground" that both sides can agree to.

But the fairness of "splitting the difference" rests on a hidden assumption: that both sides have made "final" offers that are equally distant from their theoretical "best possible" offers. Additionally, there's a hidden assumption of balance: that both sides made symmetrically fair initial offers, and have made equally fair progress toward that theoretical "best possible" offer.

In reality, though, one or both of these hidden assumptions may not be true, and, if they're not, then splitting the difference can come back to bite you. If you sense an imbalance to the call for "splitting the difference," try one or all three of these techniques:

1 Call for an impartial evaluation or appraisal. If there's no agreement between the negotiating parties regarding what constitutes a fair middle ground, get an opinion from an impartial expert. For real estate, cars, boats, and other such property, there are highly trained appraisers. In other areas, you'll have to search for impartial experts a little more creatively.

2 Let the other side argue for "splitting the difference" on price or quantity while you work toward gaining more meaningful concessions and advantages in every other area of the agreement.

3 Of course, you can also refuse to agree to "splitting the difference" if the resulting arrangement works out manifestly unfair to people on your side of the table.

CASE IN POINT

Suppose your company is looking to acquire a piece of property with the asking price of $2 million. An appraiser has listed the fair price for the property at $1 million. After hard bargaining, you offer the owner $800,000, but instead of asking a symmetrically high $1,200,000, she is still asking for $2 million. Splitting the difference would lead to a property price of $1,400,000— far more than the fair market value of the piece!

SELECTION AND ADJUSTMENTS OF COMPARABLE S...

EXPOSED TO THE MARKET AT THE SAME TIME. IN A SUBJECT'S IMMEDIATE VICINITY OR SUBDIVISION WER COMPARABLE SALES WERE NOT AVAILABLE FROM TH VICINITY OR SUBDIVISION THEN, SALE WHICH WER ...OD APPRAISAL PRACTICE), WERE MO...

...WERE MADE TO REFLECT THE DIFF ...TY AND THOSE PROPERTIES USED AS N ...ENTS WERE BASED ON THIS APPRAIS ...RKET, DATA EXTRACTED FROM THE ...AND ESTIMATED COSTS INFLUENCE ...ANDBOOK. ALL ADJUSTMENTS WE...

...STMENT FOR AGE IS BASED ON ...YSICAL DEPRECIATION BETWEEN TI ...SHOWN IN THE DEPRECIATION T ...T, TYPICAL LIFE EXPECTANCIES USED ...OF "FAIR" QUALITY, 55 YEARS FOR HON ...AND 60 YEARS FOR HOME OF ...ITY. EFFECTIVE AGES WERE ESTA ...R TABLES, ALSO IN THE MARSHALL &

...HE OPINION OF THE APPRAISER, AD. ...E NUMBER OF ROOMS IS ADEQUATELY ...UNDER GLA AND FUNCTIONAL U ...ARY, AN ADJUSTMENT WAS MADE FO. ...MBING FIXTURES IN ORDER TO COM ...BER OF BATHROOMS AND OTHER P...

...ETAILED: ADJUSTMENTS FOR ANY IT ...ALUE OF THE ITEM AT THE SUBJECT, WHEN C SIMILAR ITEM, OR LACK OF IT, AT THE COMP.

ANALYSIS OF MARKET APPROACH:

COMP #1 WEIGHTED 20%; COMP #2 WEIGHTED 30%; COMP # AND COMP #4 WEIGHTED 20% BASED ON GROSS ADJUSTMENT

1. MAXIMUM SINGLE ADJUSTMENTS TO COMPS:
   A. C#1   5.22%
   B. C#2   2.88%
   C. C#3   1.72%
   D. C#4   3.70%
   E. CONCLUSION: NO SINGLE ADJUSTMENT EXCEEDS 10%.

Property listed at $2,000,000

Appraiser lists value at only $1,000,000

You offer $800,000

SPLIT THE DIFFERENCE?

| $2,000,000 | $1,400,000 | $800,000 |

FAIR PRICE?

Maybe $1,200,000 or less . . .

RELATED TOPICS

➤ Small Concessions Can Make You a Winner, (pages 52–53)

➤ Getting Comfortable with Acceptable Risk, (pages 62–63)

Piece by Piece

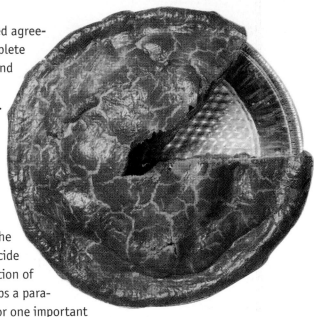

Every negotiated agreement is a complete package you and the opposing side will either accept or reject. While there's no escaping this truth, it's much more common to negotiate the agreement in small pieces.

Most of the time, the negotiating parties decide to discuss a single portion of the agreement—perhaps a paragraph in the contract or one important point such as price. You both state your positions, you make offers of concession, you ask for more from the other side, and eventually you reach agreement. Then you go on to the next item. This piece-by-piece approach can have both positive and negative consequences, depending on where you sit and what you're trying to accomplish.

Advantages of piece-by-piece negotiations

Focusing on a single issue at a time allows you to concentrate on how each possible variation will impact you and your group under a range of different scenarios.

Working on just one part of the larger agreement can allow both sides to put minor disagreements or points of contention out of sight and mind for a while. This will allow you to find common ground and gradually build up momentum toward a final agreement.

Disadvantages of piece-by-piece negotiations

Finalizing smaller parts of the agreement can have the effect of leaving both sides less "wiggle room" when major disagreements are discussed later on. For example, if you've already agreed on the price, terms, delivery dates, quality standards, quantities, and colors of an item, you have little flexibility remaining when you find each other far apart on size. The time you've spent negotiating certain parts of the agreement may go down the drain if there's another item on which neither of you will ever agree.

When you're negotiating piece by piece, never give your "final" agreement to any single issue until you're ready to sign the entire agreement. Instead, say something like, "That seems perfectly agreeable, providing we can come to terms on the other important issues that are involved here."

If you don't keep your agreements "tentative" or "interim" in this way, you run the risk of reducing your flexibility when the other side brings up an important issue you don't want to accept as the other side proposed.

The best way to gain the advantages of piece-by-piece negotiations, without risking too many of the disadvantages, is to set up a schedule of items to be negotiated. In general, it's good to begin with a simple item on the agenda, and perhaps even one on which you're willing to compromise. This sets a favorable tone for the discussions and helps establish you as a reasonable and easygoing negotiator.

After several relatively easy points, it may be time to begin negotiating on an area where both sides seem to be in major disagreement. If you can't resolve this issue and the negotiations blow apart, you haven't wasted too much time on trivia.
If you can resolve it, you've accelerated your momentum toward a final agreement.

Once over this hump, you can tackle the more difficult negotiating points one by one, interspersing simpler and less contentious issues to give both sides a breather, or to keep moving forward when people are tired, cranky, or waiting for more detailed information on a bigger issue.

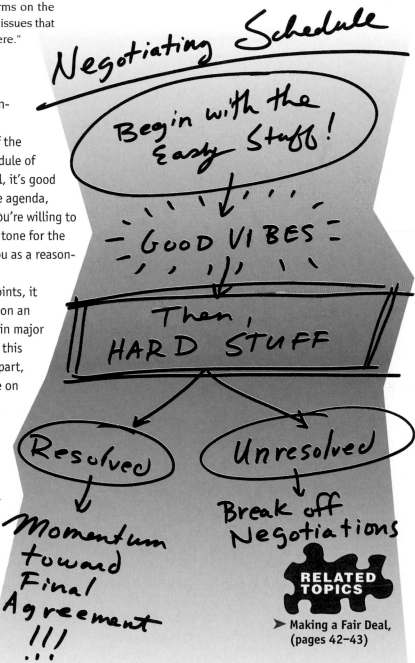

Negotiating Schedule

Begin with the Easy Stuff!

= GOOD VIBES =

Then, HARD STUFF

Resolved

Unresolved

Momentum toward Final Agreement !!!

Break off Negotiations

RELATED TOPICS

➤ Making a Fair Deal, (pages 42–43)

The Surprise Advantage

One reason for the careful preparation we've previously discussed is that a surprise revealed in the midst of delicate talks can often throw your entire negotiating position off balance.

Whether the other side makes a sudden announcement or shows an abrupt change of tactics, it can force people on your side to begin studying new figures or running new scenarios, and can even create entirely new and difficult problems that can prevent you from getting what you want.

Some of the most common surprises you're likely to encounter include:

"We've found someone who can offer a better deal than you."

"Our VP wants to talk to your VP."*

"We've changed our specifications and demands, perhaps on items previously agreed to, perhaps on items not yet discussed."

*(when neither has participated in the negotiations to date)

If the other side does spring a surprise on you, try not to react with dismay. Instead, remain calm. Get the particulars of the surprise—exactly what specifications they're changing, exactly when their vice president wants to meet with yours, and so forth. Then say something like:

"We'll take this under advisement and get back to you."

If the surprise is likely to impact the entire course of the negotiations, probably the best thing to do is stop talking, go back to your offices, and regroup. On the other hand, if the changes to be caused by the surprise are relatively limited, you might want to keep negotiating on other matters until you're ready with a response to the other side's bombshell.

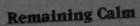

Remaining Calm

The best preparation for receiving surprise information is to remain alert during the negotiations. This way, the information may surprise you but shouldn't catch you off guard. Practice your reactions to surprise information. Consider positive ways to respond that don't indicate the panic, anxiety, and dismay you could feel in the moment. If you've already formulated calm responses to a surprise attack, you'll be better prepared to diffuse its impact.

RED ALERT! Be careful with a negotiating opponent who seems to be saving a major point of contention for the last issue. Sometimes, such a delay makes sense; but other times, it's a way to sandbag you with big demands after you've made a heavy investment of time and effort in working toward an agreement. The people across the table may hope you'll be so tired, or eager to conclude the negotiations, that at this point you'll agree to difficult terms without too much of a fight.

CASE IN POINT

In his first series of important decisions for Handey Printing, Jerome Jackson felt that he was doing well for the company. He and his opponent, Petra Pederson of Renew Paper, had found common ground on many pivotal issues. They were in the home stretch of negotiations when Petra came back from a break and announced that she couldn't sell paper to Handey at the price they had agreed to.

Jerome, obviously taken aback by this surprise, wisely said, "I don't want you to agree to anything you're not happy with. Let me go back to my managers and discuss this."

Jerome's prudence worked in his organization's favor. By temporarily concluding the negotiations, he was able to go back to his supervisors and gather their opinions on this surprise point.

His opponent, Petra, who had used this tactic to get a higher price for her product, lost the momentum she was striving for, and she ended up giving Jerome the price they had earlier agreed to.

SURPRISE

Price of product is now higher

PAUSE NEGOTIATIONS

Check with supervisors/peers

RESUME

Momentum swings back in your favor

RELATED TOPICS

➤ Control Your Side's Communication, (pages 32–33)

In America's culturally diverse marketplace, "saving face" may mean more with some individuals than simply embarrassment over a negotiating blunder. To avoid placing yourself or your opponent in an uncomfortable situation that could damage your relationship, research the business etiquette of your opponent's culture.

For example, some cultures use a conciliatory, submissive face when negotiating yet their agreeing manner may not mean that they will ultimately agree to all the issues on the table. Other cultures commonly stand up, shout, and bully to win what they want.

WORDS TO LIVE BY

"I don't know the key to success, but the key to failure is trying to please everybody."

—Anonymous

Saving Face When You're Wrong

Unless you're perfect, you're bound to make a few errors during important negotiations. You might be the one to make a mistake, or your mistake might be failing to catch an error originally made by someone else on either side of the negotiating table.

The easiest way to save face, of course, is not to lose it in the first place. In other words, try to catch and correct every error your side makes before the other side ever sees it. But this isn't always possible. Once an error gets out, your best "face-saving" response depends on how large the potential impact of the mistake.

> **Any mistake throws an obstacle in the way of an agreement, but some obstacles can be much larger than others. For example:**

➤ A mistake in figuring costs or prices can result in a significant dollar loss for your side in the negotiations.

➤ A mistake in calculating dates or time lines can mean an important item can't be delivered when needed, wanted, or promised.

➤ A mistake in interpreting complex terms may leave a loophole in the requirements you're placing on the other side's performance or, alternatively, may leave you bound to actions you can't perform.

> **Whatever the source, an error can create problems out of all proportion to its intrinsic value. For example:**

➤ If the mistake is discovered before both sides have reached an agreement, one side may feel that the newly discovered truth shows their opponent to be incompetent or inexperienced.

➤ If the mistake is discovered just as an agreement is being reached, one side may feel that the revelation is a shabby trick intentionally sprung on them to win extra concessions at the last minute.

➤ If the mistake is discovered after either a partial agreement or a finalized deal, one side may become so upset that they choose not to go through with the entire arrangement. Or one side may use the mistake as an excuse to reopen talks in anticipation of getting a better deal.

Aside from giving a sincere apology and taking a more conciliatory stance to "make things right" for the other side, here are some ways to recover from that mistake you wish you hadn't made.

For a mistake with little impact, your options include:

➤ Consider eating the loss without telling anyone.
➤ Consider revealing the mistake and offering the other side a "sweetener" to accept your recommended solution.

For a mistake with significant impact, your options include:

➤ Consider revealing the mistake, reopening the negotiations to find a solution, and offering the other side a big concession just to put them in a more reasonable negotiating mood.
➤ Consider revealing the mistake and using it as an excuse to reopen negotiations on this and other points you now feel you can adjust in your favor.

For a mistake with earth-shattering impact, your options include:

➤ Consider revealing the mistake, and asking the other side for help in solving the problem.
➤ Consider finding an excuse to break off negotiations, then coming back to the table with an approach that fixes the error without calling undue attention to it.

Preventing Errors

The more important the negotiations, the more careful you must be about mistakes. By practicing these following three items, you cut down your margin of error considerably.

- Read every word of the agreement papers at least twice.
- Run scenarios in your head or on the computer to see what they mean for you and for the other side, should the agreement go sour.
- Have someone else—a lawyer, a technical expert, even a smart friend—check the agreements, just to be sure.

RELATED TOPICS

➤ Creative Problem Solving, (pages 60–61)

Turning Around a Losing Trend

In negotiations, the momentum switches back and forth from one side of the table to the other. When you're on a roll, you'll find you can persuade the other side to make concessions you never really expected to get. But when you're having a bad day, you may not be able to win a single point for your side.

Fortunately, you don't have to ride out a losing trend. You can—and should—take steps to cut this trend short and find a way to get the negotiations flowing more toward the goals and objectives you set for them. When you spot your side of the table falling into a losing trend, try one or more of these techniques:

Shift the discussion to topics more favorable to your side.
Sometimes a losing trend begins when the other side succeeds in getting you to talk about issues where your position is weaker than theirs. Try to reverse your losing trend by talking about issues where your position is stronger than theirs.

Demand an immediate one-for-one exchange of concessions.
The easiest way to stop a losing trend dead in its tracks is to win a point for your side in the negotiations. If you insist the other side make a concession right now in return for one you offer, you might be able to shift the momentum back toward your side of the negotiating table.

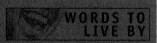

End discussions for the day.

If a coffee break doesn't stop the losing trend, you probably need more time to prepare for the opposition's tactics. An overnight or weekend break may halt your losing trend.

Find a reason to regroup.

Conceding on every point can be disastrous. Before you and your side become a casualty of a big losing streak, invent a reason to recalculate your numbers or investigate matters at a distance from the negotiating table. Take a week, or even a month, to improve your preparation and shift your negotiating team onto a more favorable track or consider rethinking this phase of negotiations altogether.

RED ALERT! Make sure you understand the difference between a losing trend and simply losing. If you find yourself in an irreversible losing trend, it's better to call off the negotiations rather than spiral downward into an agreement that will worsen your situation.

Take a coffee break.

You can't lose if you don't negotiate. When things are going badly, pause fifteen minutes for coffee, or two hours for lunch. During the break, try to get your energy level up, and your ideas and information reorganized into more persuasive form.

RELATED TOPICS

➤ After You, I Insist, (pages 50–51)

➤ Know When It's Time to Quit, (pages 72–73)

Playing Hunches and Insight

You can get a lot of mileage in many different circumstances from your intuition and the "hunches" that often result. What many people attribute to mysterious intuitive insights are really nothing more mysterious than collection and analysis of subtle clues picked up from the other side.

For example, you may very well be right when you suddenly have a hunch your negotiating opponent:

➤ Has reached the limit of his or her authority to make concessions
➤ Has remaining room in which to be flexible
➤ Is beginning to worry whether you're in a relatively stronger position
➤ Has something up his or her sleeve and is waiting for a chance to spring it on you
➤ Is ready to agree to your next reasonable proposal
➤ Doesn't really want to reach an agreement with you
➤ Is hoping you'll break off the negotiations

More often than not, these hunches contain at least a kernel of truth. Ignoring these insights and clues means you're not using all your abilities to succeed as a negotiator.

Some of these clues are easy to interpret, while others take a bit more consideration. They include:

Body Language

If your opponent has his or her arms crossed tightly, this can indicate disinterest or an unwillingness to be flexible. However, if the person's arms are on the table—or otherwise open—they too may be open to your offers.

Eye Contact

Individuals who refuse to meet your eyes may not be negotiating in good faith. But beware: an experienced negotiator knows his or her way around this clue and may meet your eyes even when they are being less than forthright.

Hand and Arm Gestures

Animated gestures indicate a willingness to show inner expression. If your opponent uses them, he or she is likely trying to persuade you into seeing the opposite side of the situation.

Nervous Movements

Like eye contact, nervous motions can often indicate more than your opponent wants to reveal. Watch for patterns of behavior, like finger tapping or foot jiggling, when you ask for a particularly large point.

Speech Patterns

An often unnoticed clue, people's speech can speed up and slow down with their level of comfort. Many people try to compensate for nervousness by filling up the silences with chatter. Note how your opponent's speech patterns vary throughout negotiations.

"If she keeps wringing her hands, I think I'll push her a little more."

"I wonder if he's really as nervous as he looks."

RED ALERT! A hunch or intuitive insight is usually a bonus, based on hard work and thorough preparation. But be wary about trying to negotiate successfully just on the strength of your hunches and intuition. No matter how lucky you have been in the past, your luck may run out when you need it the most.

Using Intuition

Don't suppress any unsubstantiated thoughts or feelings that come upon you while you're negotiating. Instead, analyze them as logically as you can to see if they might hold water.

In selected low-risk circumstances, go with your intuition. Play a hunch. Bet on your feelings instead of your thoughts. Then see how things turn out. You may get lucky. Even if you don't, the experience of actually testing your intuitive thoughts will help you refine your sense of which hunches to follow and which to ignore.

RELATED TOPICS

➤ Body Language, (pages 70–71)

Managing the Other Side's Feelings of Success

There comes a time in your growth as a negotiator when you begin to understand the importance of managing the process, as well as the content, in getting what you want. One of the most important aspects of the negotiating process is each side's feelings of progress toward their goals. Normally, these feelings ebb and flow quite naturally. Negotiators and support staff for both sides are constantly assessing how well they're doing. When they feel they've displayed some compelling facts or dismembered the other side's arguments, they go home feeling very good and contemplating a favorable agreement. When the other side seems to be winning, they feel disappointed and start considering how much they'll have to give the other side.

This ebb and flow is the mechanism by which managing the other side's feelings of success can help you gain a big advantage for people on your side of the negotiating table.

Use the following to work the other side's emotions so they help you get more from the potential agreement:

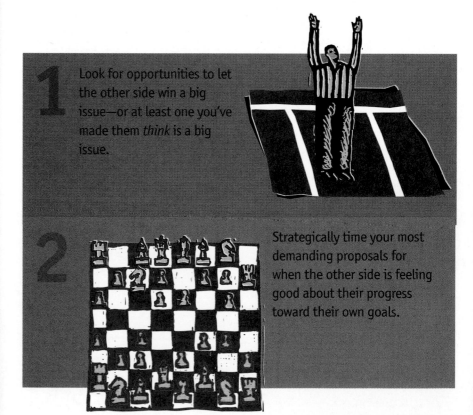

1 Look for opportunities to let the other side win a big issue—or at least one you've made them *think* is a big issue.

2 Strategically time your most demanding proposals for when the other side is feeling good about their progress toward their own goals.

3 Find opportunities to stonewall the other side on what they believe is a big issue—regardless of its importance to you.

Observe your own feelings of success. Don't get so giddy you give away the farm after what you think is a big victory. And try to pay attention to whether people on the other side of the negotiating table are manipulating your emotional state to their own advantage.

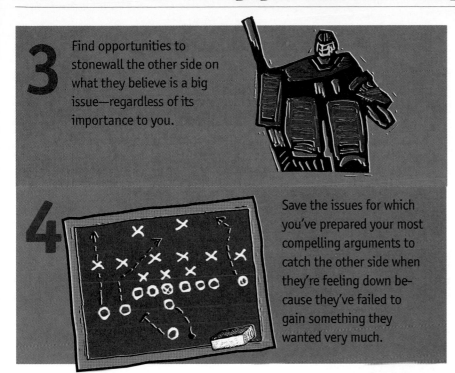

4 Save the issues for which you've prepared your most compelling arguments to catch the other side when they're feeling down because they've failed to gain something they wanted very much.

CASE IN POINT

It's been a long, drawn-out period of negotiations for Carmel Stein and his team at American Paper. Although they've been getting just about everything they need from their opponent, the Norte Lumber Corp., Carmel senses that his opponent is becoming less motivated to negotiate because it lost a couple of major points.

Because this negotiation is important to American, Carmel reviews his list of demands from Norte and decides on several small- to mid-range items that his company could part with. He then opens the next segment of negotiations by asking for a minor point in exchange for giving up what his opponent views as important.

Norte accepts this exchange and, with heightened enthusiasm, continues the negotiations. From this point on, Carmel manages the negotiation process more effectively, conceding to his opponent on points that American can easily give up. By doing so, he facilitates his own cause and gives his opponent motivation for staying in the game.

Unmotivated Opponent

You Decide on Small Concessions

Concede Small Points to Other Side

Motivated Opponent Continues Negotiations

RELATED TOPICS

➤ Stonewalling, (pages 76–77)

Your Position Improves

Glossary

Assertion—An idea, fact, or other statement presented without authoritative underpinnings and which, therefore, may or may not be accurate.

Bluffing—The act of pretending to be in a stronger position than you really are. Bluffing is difficult to accomplish and may backfire if your bluff is discovered by the other side.

Bombshell—A surprise addition to the negotiation of new information, facts, or demands that significantly changes the situation, often to your detriment.

Brinkmanship—The process of maintaining a high-risk stance in a negotiation, with little margin for error. It often leads to an either/or situation in which negotiations succeed or fail based on a single decision by one of the parties.

Communication—The most important tool used in negotiations. Your words, facial expressions, body language, and actions all communicate information to your opponent across the negotiating table. Controlling this communication is vital if negotiations are to be successful.

Compromise—The process of trading concessions on one or two items under discussion, so that neither side gets everything originally requested but both sides are satisfied with the negotiated outcome.

Concession—The agreement to a condition you originally didn't want, generally without getting any equivalent or compensating agreement from the other side.

Conciliation—The agreement to a condition the other side wants in order to make them feel better about the negotiation process.

Consensus—The condition when all parties to a negotiation (on one side or on all sides) can agree to an item or situation. If even one party disagrees, there is no consensus.

Counteroffer—An immediate response to an offer in a negotiation. It may cover the same item or a different one. For example, an offer may be "Give us $1 an hour more in salary." One possible counteroffer to this may be "We'll pay 50¢ an hour more." Another possible counteroffer: "OK, but only if you work 40 hours a week without overtime."

Deadline—A target date for completion of the negotiation, or a phase of the negotiation, often established to put added pressure on the parties to reach an agreement.

Expectation—One or both party's anticipated outcome of some or all of the negotiations. An accurate expectation can be helpful; an inaccurate one, however, can lead to disappointment or other undesirable consequences.

Fairness—The operating principle of most successful negotiators that is most easily judged by how evenly all sides are treated under the terms of the agreement.

Fatigue—The heavy-limbed, slow-witted condition that often occurs after long hours of difficult thinking or talking. It's important to be on guard against fatigue, because it is counterproductive to successfully negotiating for what you want.

Hardball—A reference to major league baseball, where a misthrown pitch or mishit ball can result in serious injury, and where only the best can cope with the pressures and competition. "Playing hardball" generally means not missing any opportunity to gain an advantage over the other side.

Intimidation—The feeling that one side is more powerful or more capable of inflicting harm than the other. Some negotiators routinely use intimidation as a tool to obtain the best deal for their side. Some people are more susceptible to intimidation than others.

Negotiable—A situation or condition that can be discussed and modified to satisfy all parties involved. A common expression is: "Everything is negotiable."

Non-negotiable—A situation or condition that one side feels strongly should not be modified in any way. Non-negotiable demands are the most common obstacles to successful negotiations.

Orchestrated—Controlled and prepared so as to work out better for your side. Orchestrated remarks, demonstrations, and negotiating sessions can all be used to lead the other side to feel more comfortable giving you more of what you want.

Rebuttal—An argument used to oppose, refute, or discount the other side's point of view and supporting information.

Secrets—The underlying content and ammunition often considered much more valuable by virtue of being unknown to some of the participants in negotiations. Secrets can include private decisions on what concessions to make, private research on the value of certain conditions, and private discussions between negotiating parties.

Socratic method—The process of asking a series of questions, the answers to which lead to a specific idea or conclusion that the questioner wants to convey.

Stonewalling—The act of steadfastly refusing to change one's mind or listen to any new ideas. Many negotiators stonewall as a method of getting the other negotiating side to be satisfied with less.

Strategy—The main attitude, arguments, facts, and overall approach to be used in a particular negotiation or against a particular negotiating opponent. Having the right strategy often produces successful results in negotiations.

Strength—The condition of being able to obtain what you want from many different sources, so that reaching an agreement with one particular party is fairly unimportant.

Subagreements—The various aspects of a complex agreement that can be negotiated separately and completed before the final agreement.

Sweetener—A last-minute, often unrelated, addition to negotiated terms intended to make the other side more willing to agree. For example, "If you agree right now, I'll take us all out to dinner at the finest restaurant in town."

Tough-minded—The character trait or quality possessed by a negotiator who seems utterly determined to win his points and get his way—no matter how strongly the other side tries to dissuade him or her. Tough-minded negotiators are not easily distracted, intimidated, bluffed, or cajoled into concessions they don't want to make.

Weakness—The condition of being able to obtain what you want only from one or two different sources, so that reaching an agreement with one particular party is relatively vital.

Wiggle room—The flexibility to rethink and restate points made earlier so as to, in effect, reopen parts of the negotiation the other side may have thought were completed. The less wiggle room you leave the other side, the better.

Resources

Associations and Websites

American Marketing Association: http://www.ama.org/
Offers links to member sites and marketing newsgroups, access to info centers, conferences, directories, on-line services, and industry publications.

Useful Organizations and Societies: http://www.ntu.ac.sg/~ctng/assoc.htm
One of the most comprehensive and up-to-date directories of major business, scientific, engineering, and educational societies on the Web.

Yahoo Business Organizations: http://www.yahoo.com/Business_and_ Economy/Organizations/
Best and most link-heavy directory of business organizations. Over twelve organizational categories—including business development, consortia, foundations, professional organizations, international trade, with brief descriptions at each listing.

Books

Communicating at Work—Improve Your Speaking, Presentation, and Correspondence Skills to Get More Done and Get What You Want at Work. Tony Alessandra, and Phil Hunsaker, New York: Fireside, 1993.

Friendly Persuasion: How to Negotiate and Win. Bob Woolf. New York: Berkeley Books, 1990.

Getting Past No: Negotiating with Different People. William Vry. New York: Bantam Books, 1991.

Getting to Yes—Negotiating Agreement Without Giving in. Roger Fisher, William Vry, and Bruce Patton. New York: Penguin, 1991.

Getting What You Want—How to Reach Agreement and Resolve Conflict Every Time. Kare Andersen. New York: Plume, 1993.

Negotiating for Your Life: New Success Strategies for Women. Nicole Shapiro. New York: Henry Holt, 1993.

On Negotiating. Mark H. McCormack. Beverly Hills: Dove Books, 1995.

Persuasive Communication. Erwin P. Bettinghaus and Michael J. Cody. New York: Holt, Rinehart & Winston, Inc., 1987.

The Power of Persuasion: A Guide to Moving Ahead in Business and Life. G. Ray Funkhouser. New York: Times Books, 1986.

The Power to Persuade—How to Be Effective in an Unruly Organization. Richard N. Haass. Boston: Houghton Mifflin, 1994.

Roger Dawson's Secrets of Power Negotiating. Roger Dawson. Franklin Lakes, N.J.: Career Press, 1995.

Secrets of Successful Speakers: How You Can Motivate, Captivate, and Persuade. Lilly Walters. New York: McGraw-Hill, 1993.

You Can Negotiate Anything. Herb Cohen. New York: Bantam Books, 1980.

Winning When It Really Counts: Quick Strategies for Success in Any Speaking Situation. Arch Lustberg. New York: Simon & Schuster, 1988.

World-Class Negotiating: Dealing in the Global Marketplace. Donald W. Hendon, and Rebecca Angeles Hendon. New York: John Wiley & Sons, 1990.

Magazines

Business Week (800) 635-1200

Entrepreneur—the Small Business Authority (800) 274-6229

Fortune (800) 621-8000

Inc.—the Magazine for Growing Companies (800) 234-0999 or (303) 604-1465

Sales and Marketing Management (800) 821-6897

On-line Services

America Online: (800) 827-6364, e-mail address: http://www.blue.aol.com/

Compuserve: (800) 848-8990, e-mail address: http://www.compuserve.com/

Prodigy: (914) 448-8000, e-mail address: http://www.prodigy.com/

Other Books in the Series

First Books for Business provide answers to your most pressing questions. In developing this series, we brought together an expert panel of top-notch businesspeople who shared their flair for success.

We know that the business world is chaotic and your time is valuable. So, we have taken the best of this panel's expertise and now present it in 50 colorful two-page chapters. Read it from cover to cover or use it as a reference guide. Either way, *First Books for Business* is your roadmap to business success.

Budgeting and Finance

To work effectively in today's marketplace, you must understand the importance of keeping projects "within budget." *Budgeting and Finance* demystifies the often confusing terms and paperwork associated with financial matters. This guide makes budgeting and finance principles easy to understand and will help you jump into the budget process with confidence. You'll learn how to:

- Understand your organization's budgetary needs
- Collect information to create a budget
- Read a financial statement
- Work with others to develop a budget that works
- Interpret what budget and finance figures say about an organization

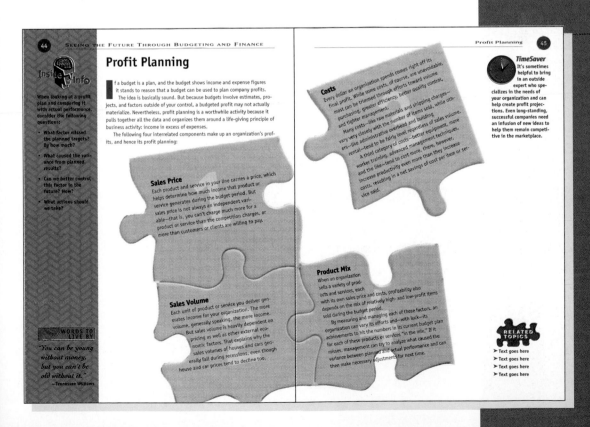

Business Presentations and Public Speaking

Knowing how to make a powerful presentation is the key to getting your point across in any business situation. *Business Presentations and Public Speaking* will show you how to increase the effectiveness of your presentation, whether in informal staff meetings or large conferences. You'll learn how to:

- Prepare an interesting, thorough presentation
- Capture your audience's attention
- Tell your audience what they want to know
- Sell them on yourself and your service or product
- Budget your time

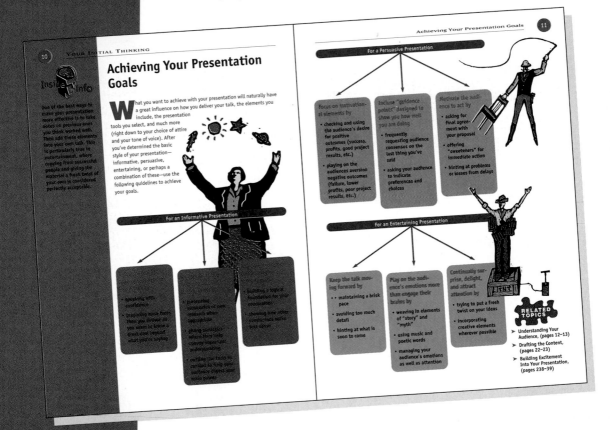

Sales and Marketing

Effective sales and marketing is key to the success of any business. *Sales and Marketing* sets forth the fundamental tools you need to effectively position your business. This user-friendly guide will show you how to create a marketing budget, perform research, and conduct marketing based on your organization's specific needs. You'll learn how to:

- Determine goals and objectives of your marketing
- Identify and plan the strategy for reaching your markets
- Execute a tailormade marketing campaign
- Evaluate the overall success of your efforts

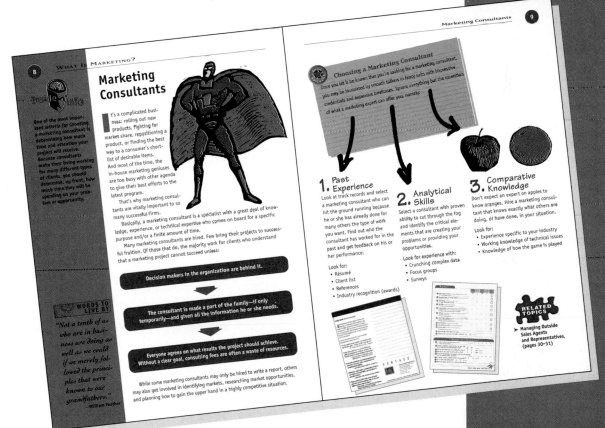

Supervising and Managing People

Whether you supervise one or many, effective management will build your confidence and help you make your organization more productive. *Supervising and Managing People* offers smart, commonsense guidance for motivating and guiding your employees through both the short and long term. This handbook makes sense of the many issues that can arise between a supervisor and employees, from creating a mentor system to creative problem solving. You'll learn how to:

- Interview and hire the best individual for each job
- Work with employees to enhance goodwill and increase productivity
- Understand the many legal issues of management in the workplace
- Deal with issues such as verbal abuse and sexual harassment
- Motivate and guide employees to be their best

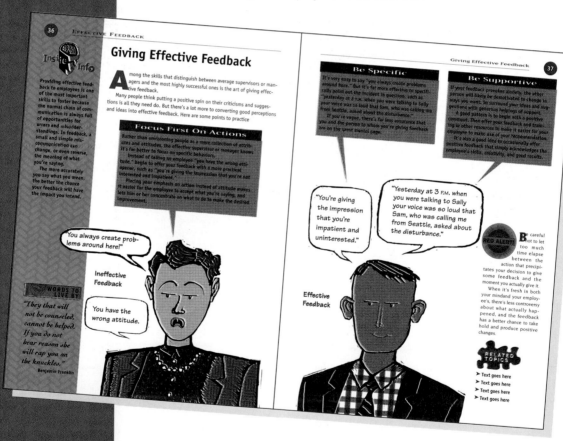

Index

Acceptable risk, 62–63
Adjustments, making, 39
Adversarial encounter, 36
Adversarial tone, 26
Agenda, 59
Aggressive style, 49
Agreement, failure to reach, 26
Alertness, 25
    maintaining, 31
    of opponent, 30
Analytical style, 48
Answers, getting, 27
Arbitration, 17
Argument, persuasive, 28–29

Backpedaling, 87
Bargaining incentive, 44
Bargaining, fairness and, 42
Biorhythms, 10–11
    timing and, 41
Blackmail, 83
Bluffing, 78–79
Body language, 11, 70–71
    insight and, 99
Business cycles, timing and, 40

Calmness, 93
Changing the subject, 5
Circumstances, timing and, 40
Coffee breaks, 97
Communication
    control of, 32
    effective, 22–23
Communication skills, 32–33
Compromise, 3
Compromise position, 7
Concessions
    advantage of small, 52–53
    exchange of, 96
    list of, 64
    order of, 10–11

    timing and, 65
    when to offer, 53
Conciliation, 64–65
Context of negotiation, 16–17
    and fulfilling expectations, 39
Conversation, process of, 24
Creative locks, 61
Current negotiation, reason for, 16

Deadlines, 34–35
Debate, 66–67
Demands,
    listing your, 6
    making your, 5
Demonstration, 31

Errors, saving face and, 94, 95
Expectations, 17
    being reasonable about, 36–37
    fulfilling your, 38–39
    ranking your, 38
    stonewalling and, 77
External factors, 27
External pressure, 17
Eye contact, 99
Eyes, ability to focus, 12

Facial expression, 71
Fact, assertion of, 28
Fairness, 42–43
    process of, 43
Fatigue, 12
Flexibility, 2–3
    stonewalling and, 77
Focus
    and debate, 67
    of eyes, 12
    listening and, 25
Follow-up, 27

Gestures, insight through, 99

Give one, get one approach, 21
Goals
    concessions and, 10, 52–53
    defining your, 6–7
    focusing on, 58–59
Good faith bargaining, 85
Guessing game, 37

History of negotiations, 14, 27
Home court advantage, 44–45
Hospitality, 45
Hot buttons, 29
Hunches, 98–99

Idealistic style, 49
Impartial evaluation, 88
Important issues, list of, 5
Inclusive style, 49
Industry trends, 14
Inside information, 19
Insight, 98–99
Intelligent listening, 24–25
Intimidation, 15, 82–83
Intuition, 99
Issues, non-negotiable, 4

Lighting, and conference setting, 56
Limb position, and body language, 71
Listening. See also Intelligent listening
    reflection and, 24
    win-win approach and, 3
Logic, persuasion and, 69
Losing trend, 96

Marathon sessions, 15
Meals, and conference setting, 57
Minor points of negotiation, 22
Mirroring, 70
Mistakes, saving face and, 94, 95
Misunderstanding, of position, 23, 67
Momentum, timing and, 41
Money, and expectations, 37

Negotiation targets, 7
Negotiation, termination of, 15, 72–73
    and walking away, 86
Non-negotiable items, 4–5

Objectives
    mutual, 2
    of opponent, 14, 27
Opponent, 14–15
Options, and expectations, 37
Organizational strengths, 14
Overdocumentation, 29
Ownership, and expectations, 37

Pacing yourself, 44
Past negotiations, records of, 9
Paying attention, 25
Persistence, 26
Personal negotiating style, 48–49
    of opponent, 15
Personal points, 31
Personal space, 83
Persuasion, 28–29, 68–69
Persuasive argument, 28–29
Persuasive style, 48
Physical harm, threats of, 83
Piece-by-piece negotiations, 90–91
    final agreement and, 91
Place cards, 57
Posture, 70
Power, and expectations, 37
Previous contact between negotiators, 14
Problem solving, 60–61
Process of fairness, 43
Process of negotiation, 17
    management of, 100–101
Professional mediator, 21

Ranking your expectations, 38
Reflecting on a concept, 24
Regrouping, 97
Reputation
    building your, 66

of opponent, 15
Research, 15
    and context of negotiations, 16
Response, holding back, 20, 25
Responsibilities, and expectations,
    37
Results, 10
Reward, persuasion and, 69
Rights, and expectations, 37
Risk, tolerance for, 63
Role-playing, 39
    good guy/bad guy type of, 74–75

Sabotage, 33
Saving face, 94–95
Schedule of negotiable items, 91
Scheduling, and conference setting,
    57
Seasonal changes, timing and, 40
Seating, and conference setting, 56
Self-discipline, body language and,
    11
Self-monitoring, 55
Setting, of negotiations, 56–57
Shouting, 30
Silence, 5
    power of, 50
Sleep, 44
Small concessions, 52–53
Socratic method, 67
Speech patterns, insight through, 99
Splitting the difference, 88–89
Stonewalling, 76–77
Strategic advantage, 50
Strategy
    for fulfilling expectations, 39
    for win-win approach, 3
Straw man, 67
Strength, negotiating from, 18
Structure, of debate, 67
Sucker, 36
Surprise advantage, 92–93

Tactics, of opponent, 14, 27
Team captain, 13
Team consensus, 32–33
Team loyalty, 32–33
Team negotiations, 13
Telephone, 46–47
    low security of, 47
Temper, 80–81
    examples of bad, 81
    strategies for dealing with bad, 80
Termination, 15, 72–73
Terms, agreement with, 19
Time log, 13
Time of day, and body clock, 10–11
Timing, 40–41
    holding back and, 51
Trade-offs, 20
Trust, persuasion and, 68

Ultimatums, 84–85

Vague promises, 27
Videotaping, 33
Visualization, 13
    risk and, 63
Vital information, 24
Voice, tone of, 71

Weak position, 8–9
    of opponent, 18
    strengthening of, 9
Weakness
    exploitation of opponents, 14
    negotiating from, 18
    vital information and, 24
Whispering, 30
Win-win approach, 2–3
    strategy for, 3
Worst-case scenario, 54–55
    matrix of, 55

Credits

Illustration

Ampersand: 75; Art Parts: 6, 11, 25, 32, 33, 42, 46, 50, 57, 61, 62, 68, 69, 72, 73, 80, 84, 85, 88, 89, 100, 101; Frank Loose Design: 12, 13, 14, 15, 20, 21, 44–45, 76–77, 81, 86–87, 94, 96–97, 98; Image Club Graphics: 2, 8, 30, 31, 44 top, 54, 60, 65, 82, 83; Rick Pinchera: 18, 19

Photography

Digital Stock Corporation: 56 top; Digital Wisdom, Inc.: 4, 5, 24, 66, 71, 74, 99; Image Club Graphics: 9 left, 9 right, 38, 43, 48, 49; PhotoDisc: 7, 9 center, 22, 28, 29, 40, 41, 78, 90; Softkey: 58

Notes